SUFFERING IN 3-D

SUFFERING IN 3-D

Connecting the Church to Disease, Disability, and Disorder

John C. Kwasny, Ph.D

COUNSEL FOR THE HEART

A RESOURCE for WORD-BASED TRANSFORMATION and PRACTICAL DISCIPLESHIP

Shepherd Press
Wapwallopen, Pennsylvania

© 2019 John C. Kwasny, Ph.D

ISBN
Paper: 978-1-63342-167-7
epub: 978-1-63342-168-4
Kindle: 978-1-63342-169-1

Shepherd Press
P.O. Box 24
Wapwallopen, PA 18660

www.shepherdpress.com

Page design by **documen**

Appreciation for *Suffering in 3-D*

I cannot overstate the timely importance and helpfulness of this book as the church presses on together in the Biblical Counseling movement. John Kwasny skillfully articulates a 21st century response to human suffering that joins together our compassionate God and the many lives marred by disability, disease and disorders. John walks a line in this book that is not traveled often enough: he articulates the depth of suffering and yet does so in a way that demonstrates the Scriptures' competence to speak to such things; he affirms the complexity of suffering, yet confirms that we are far more than a disability, disease or disorder in the eyes of our Creator and Redeemer.

Chase Maxey, Executive Director & Counselor
Biblical Counseling and Training Ministries.

John Kwasny does an excellent job of calling the church to care for some of its most needy and neglected members. He wisely brings together his extensive practical experience with careful biblical exposition as he seeks to mobilize the church to welcome and serve the weak among us. He asserts that "every local church needs a disability ministry." He also calls us to allow them to use their unique gifts to bless and serve us so that the church can be for each person "a place to belong as a member of God's redeemed people."

Jim Newheiser, Director of the Christian Counseling Program and Associate Professor of Counseling and Practical Theology, Reformed Theological Seminary Charlotte, NC.
Executive Director of The Institute for Biblical Counseling and Discipleship.

John practices what he writes. He is a generous and compassionate pastor-counselor who contributes to the beautification of the body of Christ as he sees and includes those with different kinds of suffering. He will help you and your church to do the same.

Edward T. Welch, Ph.D., Faculty and counselor at the Christian Counseling & Educational Foundation (CCEF); Author of: *Addictions: A banquet in the grave*, *Depression: Looking up from the Stubborn Darkness*, *Shame Interrupted*, and *Side by Side*

One of the many strengths of this book is that it understands suffering in light of the Gospel, and then it places the church at the center of caring for those who suffer. Kwasny looks at human suffering square in the face and responds with biblical and practical wisdom. His years of service in the context of the local church put flesh and blood on the pages. Those who suffer, those who want to help, or those who simply want to understand suffering will find wisdom here.

Miles V. Van Pelt, Ph.D., The Alan Hayes Belcher, Jr. Professor of Old Testament and Biblical Languages. Director of the Summer Institute for Biblical Languages; Academic Dean, Reformed Theological Seminary, Jackson, Mississippi.

Suffering in 3-D is a gracious gift to the Church. It is a rare blend of compassionate care and biblical wisdom rooted in the gospel, and lived out in the Christlike community of the local church. John Kwasny presents a "doable model" for culturally sensitive ministry to all who suffer common or uncommon afflictions. Every believer and local church will be blessed by reading, discussing, and applying its counsel. If I could make this required reading for church leadership teams, I would, as they will be greatly helped by working through its evaluation tools and practical helps.

Paul Tautges, DMin. Pastor at Cornerstone Community Church, Mayfield Heights, Ohio; author of many books, including *Pray About Everything, Counseling One Another, Comfort the Grieving,* and *Discipling the Flock*; Series Editor, LifeLine Mini-books.

DEDICATION

First and foremost, this book is dedicated to my
incredible wife, Martie, whose initial searching
questions about the practical difference between
disability and disorder challenged me to begin this
effort. She was (and is) my biggest cheerleader
and inspiration from day one to the very end.
Her endless, energetic work and leadership in
disability ministry is absolutely amazing; so, too,
is her sacrificial love as my helpmate and closest
companion in this crazy life of ours.

A big thanks also to Bryan for his relentless efforts
to get this book published, and for his desire to
see Biblical counseling more deeply connected to
disability ministry.

And to one of my biggest fans and supporters,
Paula, who was the manuscript's first serious
reader—time and time again!

And to Joni, whose very life as a follower of
Christ Jesus is such a personal inspiration—as
well as is her longing to see all people touched by
disability receive gospel-driven, Christ-centered
Biblical counseling!

CONTENTS

Why This Book?

A biblical view of suffering in this fallen world calls the church of Jesus Christ to have a more robust understanding of the unique suffering of individuals. If we think of the person as three-dimensional (with height, width, and depth), then a helpful way to consider the various types of suffering would be the use of a 3-D paradigm. These three distinct—yet overlapping—"D" categories of human suffering are: disease, disability, and disorder. For the church to *care* for people in a complete 3-D manner, it must become fully *connected* to the 3-Ds of disease (the absence of ease), disability (the absence of ability), and disorder (the absence of order). This will enable Christians to live out the exhortation of the apostle Paul: "If one member suffers, all parts suffer with it . . ." and ". . . but that the members may have the same care for one another" (1 Corinthians 12:25,26). Caring for all who suffer with any of the 3-Ds requires the church function as a hospital, a family, and a discipleship culture.

THE CHURCH AS . . .

As you read this book, you will find the church often being described as a hospital, as a family, and as a discipleship culture. To keep these ideas clearly in focus, the first two terms are usually rendered in hyphens to intentionally underscore this thought in the minds of readers, thus "the-church-as-hospital" and "the-church-as-family."

FOREWORD

BEFORE YOU BEGIN . . .

When I broke my neck in a 1967 diving accident that severed my spinal cord, I instantly became a quadriplegic. With arms and legs hanging limp and useless, I had to face life in a wheelchair. I didn't like it one bit, and within a few months, I sank into a deep depression.

I was a Christian at the time, but God seemed far off and uncaring and unfeeling. I knew that the Bible probably contained answers for my plight, but I had no idea where to look. I felt like gagging when I read, "Count it all joy when you face trials," or "Rejoice in suffering." None of it resonated. But I could not continue living with such hopelessness.

Thankfully, Christians were praying, and that meant God was getting ready to change things. He brought by a young man, Steve Estes, who knew nothing about disabilities, but had a solid grasp of the Bible. "Would you like to get out of depression?" he asked. "Do you want to move forward rather than feel stuck in the past?" His questions raised my hopes and so, with wet eyes, I nodded yes. Steve agreed to come by my house and help me find answers in the pages of Scripture.

True, I had to act on Steve's counsel and become a doer, and not a hearer, of God's Word, but as hope became large in my heart, it was just too wonderful not to pursue. I was convinced the Bible did indeed contain the answers to my deepest longings.

And now, decades later, I'm still convinced the Bible is sufficient to help thousands like me, whether it's a broken neck, broken heart, or a broken home. I also believe there are many Christians like my friend Steve who want to intervene and break the cycle of despair among people who suffer life-altering injuries or illnesses, or who have children with multiple disabilities. They just need a little help.

It's because things are a little more complicated than when I broke my neck in 1967. A spinal cord injury is easy to diagnose, but now, there are countless autoimmune disorders which don't even have a name. Then again, there are names that make you wonder, such as *Oppositional Defiant Disorder*. What does *that* mean?

Christians like Steve—whether lay persons, pastors, or credentialed biblical counselors—need a clearer understanding of the culture of disability and its unique facets. If the church wants to be relevant in today's world of disability, Christian leaders must acquire a better handle on the changing landscape of disability definitions and classifications. Different disabling conditions require different approaches.

It's why *Suffering in 3-D* is so needed. I consider it groundbreaking and, perhaps, controversial since its ideas are so cutting edge. Even provocative. But I'm convinced there is truth within the following pages which can bring clarity and understanding to those who sincerely want to counsel people with disabilities with the plumb line of God's Word.

Please look at the book you hold in your hands as an insightful guide when you seek out suffering families in your congregation. They won't find hope in bureaucratic institutions, service providers, or in offices of secular psychiatrists. Real and lasting hope can only be found in the pages of God's Word and among God's people. I know... I suffered a life-altering medical condition... I desperately needed help... and I found hope through compassionate friends like you who follow Jesus and His Word.

Joni Eareckson Tada
Joni and Friends International Disability Center
Agoura Hills, California
November 2018

INTRODUCTION

Since the entrance of sin and death into our world, human beings have been suffering in diverse ways, from internal and external sources. At seemingly all points of human history, people have attempted to understand suffering, solve it, and help fellow sufferers. In the time in which we live, it can often appear that the types of human suffering are ever-expanding and proliferating: physically, mentally, emotionally, spiritually, and relationally. It may be that we are just becoming more and more aware of all our suffering—and more connected to other people's suffering. Or, with the complex times we live in, it might also be that we have become much more complicated as human beings. Whatever the case, it is clearly a God-glorifying activity to be actively understanding our own suffering, the suffering of others, and entering in to others' suffering in a Christ-centered, gospel-driven, and helpful way.

As Christian ministers, servants, and helpers, an essential element of the understanding of the complexity of suffering is to ensure that we see humans as three-dimensional beings—in the sense of describing people in well-rounded completeness. This 3-D understanding connects us to the vital suffering categories of disease, disability, and disorder and how they interact with one another. These broad umbrella terms for our suffering can be used as starting points for understanding ourselves and caring for one another in the church. Labels and diagnoses that are received from other helpers and professionals, as well as ones that are self-applied, can describe much about how we are specifically struggling at the time. Yet, they can also become less than helpful, and keep us from proper care, cure, and change, if they are somehow disconnected from a biblical worldview of suffering.

In the end, we are to see the suffering of others in a holistic, or complete way. We are body and soul, not just a complex of biology and chemistry. We are physical, but we are also spiritual. We are mind and brain, heart and spirit, outward and inward. We are our genes, as well as our history and experiences. To not connect all our suffering together gives us incomplete pictures and simplistic definitions. We have diseases that are disabling. We have disorders that are caused by disease. We have disabilities that lead to disorders. And they all come in very unique packages called a person! Recognizing our similarities allows us to make diagnoses and create categories. Understanding our differences enables us to give God glory for how unique every one of His creatures truly is. Distinctions and connections will give us a more robust model of care of those God brings into our lives.

Yet, the local church is not just a humanitarian organization, self-motivated and independently working to care for suffering people. Instead, Christians take our cue and our charge from the magnificent power and glory of God, who is always at work in the lives of sufferers. In Scripture, we constantly read of how God the Father sees His people's affliction and knows their sufferings (Exodus 3:7). God the Son is moved by compassion for His suffering sheep, and is our ultimate and perfect fellow-sufferer (Matthew 9:36; 1 Peter 2:21). God the Holy Spirit is described as the great Comforter to teach us and guide us through all our trials and tribulation (John 14:26). The church of Jesus Christ works to put the love of God for sufferers on display, motivated by that same love to care for others—acting as the hands and feet of Christ (1 Corinthians 12:27).

As we focus on this effort, the apostle Paul captures well what the local church's view of helping people should be: "And let us not grow weary of doing good, for in due season we will reap, if we do not give up. So then, as we have opportunity, let us do good to everyone, and especially to those who are of the household of faith." (Galatians 6:9-10). When we forget that we are to care for *all* who suffer in any and every way, God's Word calls us to make the most of every opportunity. When we are fearful or frustrated in how to effectively help others, we do not give up, but persist in the grace and love of God. When we are fatigued in all our helping efforts, we are reminded that spiritual, refreshing, blessings are ours in Christ. The church is to never shrink back from caring for all who suffer, but to always hold out the person of Jesus Christ, the Suffering Servant of God, even in our own weakness (2 Corinthians 2:12).

THE CHURCH CONNECTED TO SUFFERING IN 3-D

"If one member suffers,
all the parts suffer with it . . ."

At some point in our lives—often at many points—we reluctantly become personally connected to various types of human suffering. Some of these connections are short-lived, ending with a temporal healing of a disease, or the ultimate healing found only in heaven. Other connections are more longstanding, such as a chronic disability or a pervasive mental and emotional disorder. In most cases, we are not willing participants in personal suffering, or in the suffering that occurs in the lives of those closest to us. There are many methods we may be tempted to try to employ to disconnect emotionally from the suffering in our lives—even attempting to avoid pain altogether. But God calls his children to something bigger and better. We are to responsible to enter into our own suffering, as well as the suffering of others, with biblical wisdom and a firm faith in God's sovereign and compassionate work of grace. When we are connected to pain and suffering, it is always an opportunity to grow in the image of Christ as the Suffering Servant, and grow in love for God and other people.

While connecting to suffering is a very personal and intimate activity, mindset, and process of the heart, it is also designed to be a corporate affair. As Christians, we are not to walk alone in our suffering (even though that seems to be easier), or inadvertently force others to deal with suffering on their own. The church, as the body of Christ, is to be one-minded and spiritually passionate about its charge to connect to those who suffer in the midst. The local church is to recognize and have a biblical understanding of the pervasiveness of suffering all around. It is to properly deal with all of the common obstacles to a right grace-based relationship with all those who suffer. And ultimately, the church is not to just tolerate or endure sufferers in its midst, but welcome, pursue, and embrace sufferers as full members of the body of Christ. With these biblical goals in mind, Part One of

Suffering in 3-D details the call to connect to suffering in the church so that the church may fully participate in God's work of serving and ministering to all who suffer from disease, disability, and disorder.

CHAPTER 1

THE PERVASIVENESS OF SUFFERING

A 3-D View of Suffering in the Church

Most of our modern churches employ some sort of system to communicate prayer requests to the congregation. Some still have a "prayer and praise" section in the weekly church bulletin. Many others use email, text, or social media to send out personal requests so that church members can pray more immediately. If we did a random survey of churches which practiced some sort of prayer chain, what would we find to be the most common types of prayer requests? My guess for things that would make the shortlist would be: loved ones in the hospital, newly diagnosed cases of cancer or other life-threatening diseases, births and deaths, and other sorts of crises. Whatever typically makes it on these prayer request lists and prayer chains, these communications provide the congregation with vital information about members who are suffering

What if some of your church members wanted to request prayers from the entire congregation for other sorts of issues? Peggy wants everyone to pray that her autistic son would start sleeping more than his usual one hour a night. Albert desires the church to pray for his frequent panic attacks and generalized anxiety disorder. Philip needs prayer for his porn addiction. Louise asks the church to pray for her communication and conflict struggles with her husband. Leah longs for her fellow members to pray for her son's ADHD and its impact on her family. Finally, Paige wants prayer for the hopelessness she feels for her future—due mainly to her intellectual disabilities. So, what would these sorts of "unorthodox" prayer requests communicate about your church, and to the members of your church? Would it feel way too risky, opening the church up to gossip, and these individuals and families to rejection? Or would remarkable care, compassion, and sacrificial love become a real possibility?

I hope you see the point. There is a lot more suffering going on in our churches than typically makes it on the prayer chain. While that may sound obvious, it's tempting for us to think that a short prayer request list means that all is (mostly) well with our brothers and sisters in Christ. To put it in positive terms, our local churches must embrace the truth that suffering is pervasive in the pews. We are responsible to wrap our minds around all the types of suffering among us. Only then can we move to discover how best the church can help in all dimensions of suffering. But before we dive headlong into a more comprehensive understanding of how our church members are suffering, we should start with a brief scriptural foundation of *why* human beings are suffering so much.

LIFE IN A FALLEN WORLD

You don't have to live long in this world to come to some sort of conclusion regarding the pervasive nature of human suffering. Even an avowed atheist like Richard Dawkins sees it:

> *The total amount of suffering per year in the natural world is beyond all decent contemplation.* . . . *In a universe of electrons and selfish genes, blind physical forces and genetic replication, some people are going to get hurt, other people are going to get lucky, and you won't find any rhyme or reason in it, nor any justice. The universe that we observe has precisely the properties we should expect if there is, at bottom, no design, no purpose, no evil, no good, nothing but pitiless indifference.*[1]

Like many people who don't operate from a Christian worldview, Dawkins' description of the problem is accurate, but his "why" is lacking. From a totally random, evolutionary view, human suffering has no rhyme or reason. It just is. And somehow all this suffering just proves there is no good or real purpose in this world.

Yet Christians know the truth as to why suffering has always been with us, and why it will not leave us until Christ returns.

The well-known evangelist Billy Graham sums it up:

> *Evil and suffering are real. . . . They aren't an illusion, nor are they simply an absence of good. We are fallen creatures living in a fallen world that has been twisted and corrupted by sin, and we all share in its brokenness. Most of all, we share in its tragic legacy of disease and death.*[2]

Being fallen creatures who live in a fallen world means that every one of us will suffer in some way—in many ways—at different points in our lives. We won't all suffer with the same things or always for the same reasons. Human beings are far too three-dimensional for a simplistic view of why we suffer and how we suffer. God's Word shows us that there are many causes and contributors to our suffering that aren't simply "selfish genes, blind physical forces . . . and luck." So before we can accurately think through the various ways we suffer, we need to recognize what lies behind.

OUR SIN

A thorough reading of the first few chapters of the book of Genesis reveals how the entrance of original sin into the world produced spiritual, emotional, mental, and relational problems. After Adam and Eve sinned, they experienced shame and guilt for the first time (Genesis 3:7, 10). Marital conflict broke out (Genesis 3:12, 16). Envy, jealousy, anger, and depression quickly followed in the first family, leading to the shocking murder of brother by brother (Genesis 4:5-9). Sin in human hearts produces sinful thoughts, attitudes, and actions that lead to all other sorts of problems. Clearly, we human beings can produce suffering in our lives from our own sinful decisions and responses. And Scripture holds us responsible for our rebellion and disobedience to God and His ways that can have a wide range of devastating consequences.

But then, in John 9, we may be surprised by an interaction between Jesus and his disciples: "And his disciples asked him, 'Rabbi, who sinned, this man or his parents, that he was born blind?'" (John 9:2) How could these spiritual men actually think that the cause of a man's blindness could be sin? Jesus answers them in verse 3: "It was not that this man sinned, or his parents, but that the works of God might be displayed in him" (John 9:3). A similar case that will be discussed later occurs in the book of Job. Upon witnessing Job's extreme suffering, his friends became convinced that his secret sins had caused all the devastating suffering of his life. So, while we acknowledge that sin is one cause of our suffering, we must also agree with God's Word (and Jesus) that sin is not always the cause of our suffering. A three-dimensional view of the person seeks to understand what else is working against us.

OUR PHYSICAL BODIES

In 2 Corinthians 4, the apostle Paul writes: "So we do not lose heart. Though our outer self is wasting away, our inner self is being renewed day by day" (2 Corinthians 4:16). Another clear cause of human suffering is the deterioration and degradation of our physical bodies. Due to the nature of the fall of our first parents into sin, we are now all born into this world with imperfect bodies. Because of this fact, it should be expected that our bodies will fail! We all get sick. If we live long enough, our physical, outer selves will end up wasting away. Even with all the wonderful technology, treatments, and medicines available today, human beings will never develop perfectly healthy bodies which last an eternity. So, it is essential that we hold to the truth that people experience devastating problems which are caused by their physiology, biology, and chemistry.

OTHER PEOPLE

Unfortunately, in a fallen world, we are sinners living among other sinners. And, what do sinful people do? Sin against one another, of course! All sorts of violence and abuse— sexual, physical, mental, emotional and verbal—can propel a person into any number of anxiety- or anger-based problems. Deep emotional and identity problems rooted in shame and false guilt can be caused by the sins of other people against us. Marital and family conflicts allow people to hurt each other in the profoundest of ways. Thus, the sinful actions of other people can truly bring untold suffering into our lives that will require significant care from other believers. So, to properly understand the certain types of human suffering, we must acknowledge the power of sinful actions taken upon the innocent. Even though people should take responsibility for their responses to the sins that other people have committed against them, those other people can certainly be the primary cause of our suffering.

OUR CIRCUMSTANCES

A young woman dives into a shallow lake, miraculously survives, and lives the rest of her life with quadriplegia and other related disabilities. While a child is enjoying a fireworks display on July 4th, he is suddenly left with severe visual and auditory impairments. A man has a skiing accident and has to have both legs amputated. These and other life circumstances that occur every day can be accurately observed as a cause of human suffering. Yet, as will be discussed in a moment, the things that most people see as "random events" that produce human suffering are never truly accidental. All the circumstances in our lives—from car accidents, to natural disasters, to all our injuries—always come under the hand of Divine Providence. Yet, in context of the church understanding and caring for people, it is helpful to recognize the place of difficult circumstances in our suffering.

OUR ENVIRONMENT

Similarly, it gives us a more robust view of human suffering when we take into account the difficult environments that surround the people in our congregation. Does growing up in utter poverty have an impact on people's hearts, minds, wills, and emotions? How about a child being raised in a home with a raging alcoholic and drug abuser? Or, what about the person in the pew behind you who was never disciplined as a child, but only spoiled to death? Clearly, these and other "nurture" sorts of issues will contribute to emotional, mental, and relational suffering. Thus, a thorough understanding of a person's family background, education, training, and all other environmental influences will certainly help us to rightly identify and tackle problems. Since we are living in a fallen world, our contexts and environments can have an adverse impact upon us.

OUR GREAT ADVERSARY, SATAN

In constant opposition to our holy, sovereign, and gracious God, Satan is determined to steal, kill, and destroy—bringing suffering into the lives of people (John 10:10). In the book of Job, we read of how Satan brings extreme suffering into Job's life, including physical disease (Job 2:4-7). In Luke 8:26-39, we are told the story of the Gadarene demoniac, possessed by Satan's demons and acting like a very modern psychotic. And, throughout the Gospels, we are shown how Jesus spent much of His time on earth combatting Satan's power over suffering people. The Devil certainly can be understood as a significant cause of our many of our physical, mental, emotional, and relational problems. As archaic as this notion may sound to many people in our world today, the Bible puts Satan squarely in the position as a major player in the realm of human suffering. He continues to even oppress God's people in their bodies and minds, in a desire to separate them from the love of God (if that were possible).

Our sovereign God

Finally, when we speak of the causes of suffering in this fallen world, Christians can sometimes become distressed or even angry about putting God on this list. After all, God is all about love, salvation, grace, and the relieving of human suffering, right? While that is certainly true, to understand suffering biblically we must submit to the truth of a God who is sovereign. Paul Tripp states: "The Bible clearly declares that God is sovereign over all things—even suffering."[3] We know that God, as Creator, designed our human bodies and minds to function a particular way. As he is the Sustainer of all things, we only breathe, live, and have our being because of our sovereign and gracious God. Because of His omnipotent love, we have our souls saved in Jesus Christ, and may even enjoy a level of health and wellness due to his hand. God is in control of all things, including our bodies and souls, the actions of other people, our circumstances, our environment, and even Satan. No suffering enters our orbit outside of God's sovereignty (Job 42:2, Psalm 135:6).

Toward a 3-D View of Suffering

A biblical view of suffering in this fallen world calls the church of Jesus Christ to have a more robust understanding of the unique suffering of individuals in this world. If we think of the person as three-dimensional (with height, width, and depth), then a helpful way to consider the various types of suffering would be the use of a 3-D paradigm. These three broad—yet overlapping—"D" categories of human suffering are: disease, disability, and disorder. All three of these types of suffering begin with the Latin prefix "dis," which in these cases mean "the absence of." Therefore, a disease produces the "absence of ease," a disability is the "absence of ability," and a disorder demonstrates the "absence of order." Now, that only gives us partial descriptions, doesn't it? Let's attempt to give each of these three D's of human suffering a bit more definition:

o A *disease* is a condition that prevents the physical body from working normally. It is typically synonymous with "illness."

o A *disability* is a condition caused by a disease or injury that damages or limits a person's physical or mental abilities. It is the condition of not being able to do something in a normal way.

o A *disorder* is a mental, emotional, spiritual, or relational condition that is not normal or healthy.

By these initial definitions, we can see how challenging it is to make good distinctions between types of human suffering, since they all say something similar about our problems. But in a helpful way, we should also consider how these broad classifications are distinguished from each other, yet also interact with each other. Diseases and disorders can be disabling. Diseases and disabilities may lead to disorders. Some problems can be described as a disease, disability, and disorder! Ultimately, our ease, ability, and order are limited by a vast array of different types of conditions. So, to move toward a three-dimensional model of suffering, let's give some more detail and illustrations of each "D."

DESCRIBING DISEASE
This first general group of human suffering is most closely connected to and manifested in our physical bodies. We tend to not think of sin as a main factor behind our diseases or blame other people for causing them. Instead, we think about how our bodies are breaking down, have been injured, or have become

unhealthy for a variety of reasons. Medical help of some sort becomes the priority when experiencing disease, as we seek a cure. When we focus on true physiological causation, it enables us to understand various diseases by recognizing their impact on different organ systems (like heart, lung, digestive tract, etc.). While there are wide disagreements of what sorts of suffering can be truly caused by a disease, many of our problems clearly can be identified in this way.

Mary was just diagnosed with breast cancer. Your grandmother has been in the hospital for a week with congestive heart failure. Juan has been told that he has Type 1 diabetes. A member of your mission team develops malaria due to a mosquito bite on the field. After months of severe migraines, Henry has been told he has a brain tumor. As mentioned at the beginning of this chapter, diseases are the most typical requests that will come to your church prayer chain. Once diagnosed, diseases have a fairly consistent treatment plan attached to them, administered by medical professionals. And, clearly, diseases are not just found in the life of the nonbeliever, or those with little faith, as some false teachers suggest. Diseases will be routinely found in your congregation as the result of weak, fallen bodies, as well as environmental and circumstantial causes. And even though we rightly rely on the medical world for care, the church is also called to suffer with and help people with diseases.

DESCRIBING DISABILITY

According to the 2010 US Census, about 56.7 million Americans have some sort of disability.[4] If you do the math, that adds up to almost one out of every five people (19% of the population) having some sort of disability. Does that match your experience in your church? The reality is that these numbers are high due to what is typically defined as a disability. For example, approximately seven million people reported in the census that their anxiety or depression was a disability. Almost 2.5 million Americans suffer from dementia or Alzheimer's disease, considering them to be disabilities. About 19.9 million people reported some difficulty lifting or grasping, which, according to the census, is technically a disability. So, even though most of us would think of disability in a more narrow sense, we have to recognize that there are far ranging types of conditions that are disabling.

So, our diseases may certainly produce some type of disability. As we will consider in a moment, disorders left unchecked can become disabling. Therefore, we should recognize how easy it is to assert that any and every form of suffering is actually a disability, especially problems that become chronic and longstanding in nature. In other words, it is tempting to come to the conclusion that *all* problems are actually disabilities because of the *disabling nature of our problems*. Yet, we will have much more helpful clarity in understanding disability with the use of three important terms: impairment, limitation, and restriction. To be *impaired* is to become diminished or "worse," (root meaning of the word) physically or intellectually. When a person experiences a *limitation* of activity, then it may make his or her condition rise to the level of a disability. Finally, when something causes a *restriction* of participation in work, play, or anything important in life, it can be considered a disability. So, for a problem to enter into the category of the "D" of disability, it will most likely produce an impairment of some kind, restrict activity, and limit involvement or participation.[5]

Since one of the universal symbols of disability is the wheelchair, we readily understand Joni, a woman suffering with quadriplegia, as having a disability. There are members of the local group home who all have some sort of cognitive limitation or diminished intellectual functioning. Mary Beth is a child in your church nursery with Down Syndrome. Paul and Joanna have a son, Tanner, who is on the autism spectrum. Two girls in your youth ministry have sensory processing disorders. Bill is hearing impaired, and his wife, Sue, has become visually impaired later in life. These folks in your congregation have "special needs" that require significant assistance from medical professions, family and friends, other caregivers, specially trained educators, and especially the family of God. Yet, at the same time, many of these sufferers may be facing a significant amount of isolation and rejection. And while many disabilities have an underlying disease, disabilities can be distinguished from disease by the chronic limitation they introduce into a person's life.

DESCRIBING DISORDER

Our third "D" category takes us much more deeply into the realm of the mental, emotional, and relational. The best place to begin to define this complicated arena of human suffering is with the use of the Diagnostic and Statistical Manual (DSM) of the American Psychiatric Association (APA). According to Dr. Michael Emlet, "Mental health professionals use the *DSM* as their defining resource for describing, categorizing, and diagnosing mental disorders."[6] Now in its fifth major iteration (DSM-5), each new revision has added a significant number of new disorders. This has brought some controversy over whether the DSM-5 and its predecessors are really classifying mental illnesses, or overreaching to include some everyday problems.[7] Yet, the growing list of disorders is instructive for the church, as it demonstrates the complex nature of the human being, body and soul. It sees that with each passing year, we modern folks have a way of creating and compiling more and more problems for ourselves and for each other.

Let's remind ourselves of our definition of disorder. *A disorder is a mental, emotional, spiritual, or relational condition that is not normal or healthy.* To be dis-ordered is to lack order, which, within a Christian worldview, means that it is out of God's created order. Human beings have been designed to function in a particular way in relationship to God, self, and other people. We are living souls who have been made in the image of God. Our own sin, our bodies, our circumstances, our environment, other people sinning against each other, and the deception of Satan can all contribute to all sorts of disorders. Yet it should be noted, too, that as we enter into the disorder category, we learn that an individual diagnosed with a disease or a disability can subsequently develop a disorder. Problems like anxiety, depression, anger, and addictions can be the mental and emotional responses to any number of physiological diseases and disorders. Disorders, then, can be rightly viewed as consequences to other significant problems, or they can also simply originate on their own.

Wilma has regular panic attacks keeping her out of worship services frequently. Since his retirement, Mike has had several major depressive episodes. Emma and Bob confide in you that their teenage son has questions about his gender identity. In your youth group, you know of at least three girls with some sort of eating disorder. A recent men's Bible study has brought multiple men forward with porn addictions. Ben and Amanda are struggling in their marriage because of Ben's substance abuse. While many of these sufferers will seek professional help outside of the church, how can the body of Christ help with disorders? As these problems certainly have a spiritual component to them, a culture of discipleship will be necessary. As Emlet asserts regarding our disorders: "The greater intensity of suffering, the greater the need to carefully study people and carefully study the Scripture in order to bring wise biblical perspective to their problems."[8]

CONNECTING DISEASE, DISABILITY, AND DISORDER

If you have ever played the classic bored-on-a-road-trip game "Twenty Questions," you have asked the most important (and traditionally the first) question: "Is it animal, vegetable, or mineral?" Asking that initial question helps you to narrow down your thinking in order to get to the answer to the game before your twenty questions are up. This demonstrates our natural tendency to want to get our heads around problems by making important distinctions between them. In many situations of life, this is not only acceptable, but proper—as in the case of distinguishing between animals, plants, or rocks. But in the case of human suffering, we must resist falling into the trap of making overly demarcated and rigid categories of problems. Unfortunately, all of our suffering doesn't fall neatly into 3-D groupings of disease, disability, or disorder. So, while thinking in these categories is a good analytical starting point, it's not where we, as thoughtful Christian helpers, want to end. We need to recognize how disease, disability, and disorder connect in the unique individuals in our congregations.

OVERLAPPING CONNECTIONS

An advertisement pops up during your favorite television show where an actor in doctor's scrubs says: "Depression is a medical condition . . . it's a *disease*." Later, you do an Internet search and read an article which states: "Depression is the world's number one *disability*." But then your friend, a counseling psychologist, asserts: "Depression is a mood *disorder* which affects millions of Americans every year." So, which is it? Is depression a disease, disability, or disorder? For people (like me) who crave all things to be either black or white, we will seek for a definitive compartmentalization. But, the truth is, example demonstrates how often our suffering overlaps. While distinction can often be helpful, certain types of problems defy tight categorization due to the three-dimensional complexity of the human being! Depression can be seen as a disease because of its impact on the body and its functioning. Depression, in its more chronic and extensive forms, can certainly be disabling. And depression is also a mood disorder, defined by a person's mental, emotional, and spiritual faculties being out of order.

Consider a similar potential case of suffering overlap— the problem of alcoholism. Some Christians bristle at the perspective of alcoholism as a disease, since its proponents often appear to reduce moral responsibility. Others reject alcoholism as simply a disorder, because it seems to make the person just sinful or morally weak, with the "easy" solution of using self-control to quit. And then, can't we also understand severe alcoholism as a form of disability, limiting and restricting a person's entire life? As much as it is good for Christians to challenge the underlying presuppositions about the disease model of alcoholism, we can also be sobered by a thought of a former alcoholic: "Whether I or anyone else accepted the concept of alcoholism as a disease didn't matter; what mattered was that when treated as a disease, those who suffered from it were most likely to recover."[9] While we may rightly disagree on how to solve the problem of alcoholism, recognizing the overlapping nature of the 3-Ds is more realistic, and potentially a more helpful view of the alcoholic.

Then there are those boys in your Sunday school class who have been diagnosed with attention-deficit/hyperactivity disorder (ADHD). Labeled as a "disorder" recognizes the fact that there are mental, emotional, and behavioral issues, demonstrating a lack of order. Yet, the history of this particular form of suffering has progressed in the direction of categorizing ADHD as a disease. Especially with the discovery of medications that reduce some of the symptoms of ADHD, for many, this definitively demonstrates that it is a type of brain disease.[10] But

ADHD is also widely recognized as a disability, especially in academic settings, because of its disabling "attention deficit" factor. So, while ADHD may be a confusing problem—which is regularly under debate—its overlapping nature actually demands that we seek to help the person three-dimensionally. It should also drive us to a more robust examination and understanding of *all* the contributing factors in the lives of these sufferers!

CAUSAL CONNECTIONS

A young woman in your congregation is diagnosed with Ehlers-Danlos syndrome (EDS), one of a group of inherited connective tissue disorders characterized by joint hypermobility, skin hyperextensibility, and tissue fragility.[11] In the past, she has talked with you about her struggle with regular panic attacks. After being diagnosed with EDS, her doctor mentioned that one of the side effects of this disease is anxiety. So, could it be that the panic attacks were partially, or even totally caused by this inherited disease? It certainly is a strong possibility! How many other physiologically-based diseases will we discover have, as a consequence, a particular mental or emotional disorder? Add to that understanding the anxious, angry, or depressed response that could come from having a disease like EDS, and we will have a more complicated form of suffering.

More research into particular disabilities is producing articles with fascinating titles like this one: "Many young adults with autism also have mental health issues."[12] In this article, the author gives example after example of young people who have been diagnosed with autism are also inclined to anxiety attacks, depression, and other more severe psychiatric disorders. He observes: "People with autism aren't immediately born anxious or with depression . . . the world is fundamentally not built for us, and people are always judging and trying to change you . . . of course that's going to cause a higher rate of anxiety and depression . . . ."[13] Thus, it shouldn't surprise us that most disabilities, with their often-isolating limitations, would produce a causal connection of mental and emotional disorders. If the church misses the fact that individuals and families touched by disabilities will also struggle with disorders, then it will fail to connect to some of the deeper heart needs.

How about mental, emotional, and spiritual disorders causing diseases? According to a recent *Time Online* article, research has "linked depression with an increased risk of conditions like stroke, diabetes and rheumatoid arthritis." The author goes on to describe how more and more researchers are connecting inflammation with both depressive disorder and other physical health problems.[14] Even though this is a relatively new advancement in our understanding of physical diseases and mental disorders, this should not surprise us as students of God's Word. We understand that God has created us as body *and* soul, whole people who suffer in mind and brain, in our inner and outer person (Genesis 2:7, 1 Thessalonians 5:23). The potential causal connection between mental and emotional disorders and severe physical disease should produce an urgent need to properly handle all our suffering biblically.

SPIRITUAL CONNECTIONS

For members of your church, it is probably relatively easy to recognize the spiritual connections to many of our disorders. Someone who is struggling with anxiety, fear, and worry will probably need to deal with his or her difficulty trusting God and maybe even a heart idol of control. Another congregant who has severe anger issues may need to differentiate the anger that is godly (justice-based) and the anger that is self-centered and self-righteous. All sorts of depressions and mood disorders will also require the person to examine his or her relationship with God, as well as the state of his or her heart. Even more severe psychiatric disorders like bipolar disorder or obsessive-compulsive disorder will likely require conversations about his or her relationship with God and responses to life in his world. Dr. Edward Welch puts it this way regarding disorders: "You will never find a psychiatric problem where biblical counsel—counsel directed to the heart—is anything less than essential."[15]

But what about the spiritual connection to those who suffer with diseases? It is understandable that the priority for a person diagnosed with a sickness or illness is to seek a medically based cure first. Yet, Christians are instructed by God's Word to see disease in the light for eternity. The apostle Paul writes, "For I consider that the sufferings of this present time are not worth comparing with the glory that is to be revealed to us" (Romans 8:18). Disease is also used by God to make his children more dependent on him and to grow spiritually. As Elyse Fitzpatrick and Laura Hendrickson sum up: "In your suffering you've begun to learn how much you need Him. . . . If he hadn't suffered in your place, you would continue to believe that life would work out if you just tried harder."[16] While the secularists of this world see the healing of the body as the only goal for our diseases, Christians call one another to understand God's purposes for all suffering. Disease is supposed to point our hearts to the ultimate healing we have in Christ, and will enjoy in heaven forever (Isaiah 53:5).

Speaking of her disability and its spiritual connection, Joni Eareckson Tada writes: "Suffering doesn't teach you about yourself from a textbook—it teaches you from experience. It empties you so that by faith you can be filled with the Spirit."[17] Even though this biblical lesson may go against the grain of some people suffering with disability, it's the mindset to which God calls all of us. So, while we should be focused on helping those with disabilities to greater accessibility in the church, we must also recognize their spiritual issues as well. This truth may be easier for us when we encounter people with physical disabilities, but what about folks with intellectual disabilities? Do we see possibilities for discipleship and spiritual growth, or treat them as if their lack of adequate intellectual faculties keeps them from the kingdom of God? Just because disability limits, restricts, and often excludes people in society does not mean that there is any more inability to be saved than those without an observable disability! Spiritual care, as offered by the church—with the gospel of grace—is for people with disabilities too.

Thinking toward a 3-D view of suffering is first rooted in a biblical view of life in a fallen world, not in some fatalistic conception of human existence. As Christians, the 3-Ds move us beyond what just finds its way into the prayer chains of our churches. It recognizes the complexity of the whole person, not reducing him or her to just a descriptive diagnosis. While the broad categories of disease, disability, and disorder help us make important distinctions, they are not meant to be used to simply put people into one of three diagnostic "baskets" of suffering.

They allow us to see just how broad and deep our suffering truly is—and in the diverse ways it manifests. As we will explore in our upcoming chapters, hopefully this conception will change how we conceive of the church and its functions. Instead of dividing us relationally, a 3-D categorization should *connect* us to one another as fellow sufferers. For as one member suffers, *"all members suffer with it"* (1 Corinthians 12:26).

For Personal Reflection

1. In order to connect to the suffering of others, begin with recognizing your own personal suffering over the past few years. Reflect on the central causes of that suffering, as well as factors that have contributed to it:

   o How have your own sinful choices impacted your suffering?

   o How has your body impacted your suffering?

   o What about the sins of other people in your life?

   o What current circumstances and environmental factors contribute to your suffering?

   o How do you conceive of what Satan is trying to do with your suffering?

   o What is God's goal for your suffering?

2. As you reflect on your own suffering, categorize it using the 3-D approach. Are you experiencing disease right now? A disability of some kind? A disorder of mind and heart? Whether you have an actual diagnosis or your own personal evaluation, think about how understanding it under one of the "D" categories helps you.

3. Take note of how your suffering can be viewed in a more three-dimensional way. If you have a physiological disease, it is probably creating a disability. A mental/emotional/ spiritual disorder may also have disabling elements to it. Your disability has the ability to provoke a disorder like anxiety, sinful anger, or depression.

For Church Assessment

1. Get a copy of your church directory. Think about each member of your congregation. What types of sufferings are in your midst?

2. What individuals or families do you need to pay more attention to in order to have a grasp of how such people are struggling?

3. From your knowledge of the members of your congregation, use the 3-Ds to assist you in how to best minister to them. This regular practice is not meant to label people or put them into some sort of diagnostic boxes, but to help think through their needs.

4. Evaluate how your members are suffering with one another. Compare and contrast those individuals and families who are being well served with those who are more isolated.

For Group Discussion

1. How would it change your church if the prayer request list began to reflect all the suffering in the congregation?

2. Why do we need to begin with a biblical understanding of life in a fallen world to properly understand human suffering?

3. What are the similarities between the definitions of disease, disability, and disorder? What are the differences?

4. What are some examples of problems that overlap between the 3-D categories?

5. What are some examples of how a form of suffering in one category can cause a further problem in another?

6. How do diseases, disabilities, and disorders connect to our relationship to God and our growth as believers?

7. How does it help the church to have a broader, connected 3-D view of suffering?

CHAPTER 2

THE PROBLEM OF SUFFERING

Overcoming Barriers in the Church

The Parkers are summoned to their assistant pastor's office for a meeting about Jake, their twelve-year-old son, who is on the autism spectrum. The pastor tearfully informs them that the elders have discussed their "difficult situation," and have decided to ask them to look for another church that can serve their needs better. Angela, who suffers with bipolar disorder, feels judged by the church, especially many of the women. She refuses to join another women's Bible study after a discussion about suffering didn't end well. Jim was diagnosed several years ago with mesothelioma due to long-term exposure to asbestos. While his church responded well to his disease in the beginning, he now just feels like an everlasting prayer request. No one has any idea of the daily struggle he faces with low energy, persistent pain, and deep grief about his loss. All three of these sufferers share one major thing in common: a deep desire for more from their churches and their brothers and sisters in Christ.

So, what is your immediate "first blush" response to these brief, but very real, vignettes? Personally, my first inclination is to defend our churches and my fellow believers, for the sake of the honor of Christ. Christians are busy. People have good intentions, even though they fail at times. The church can't be expected to meet each and every need of every person in the pew. Now, while there is truth in these sentiments, they may also simply be excuses, cop-outs, and rationalizations. People are often too busy to help others who are suffering—sometimes because their priorities are misplaced. People have good intentions, but good intentions don't always lead to righteous and loving actions. No, the church can't be expected to meet every need; but, is it systematically and responsibly doing what Christ has called his church to do? With an understanding of the pervasiveness of suffering in the church comes a biblical duty to deal with the problem of human suffering. And the first problem is: us! We have barriers to overcome first before we can serve people with diseases, disabilities, and disorders.

FACING OUR FEARS

Upon the initial diagnosis of a disease, disability, or disorder there is a vast array of possible responses. At the top of the long list is shock, especially when it is unexpected. Anger, anxiety, or despair can quickly follow. Along with these emotional responses, sufferers may also be struggling with how to think about what's happening. Maybe there's some relief to, at least, have an accurate diagnosis, prognosis, and treatment plan. Or, there can be those frustrating "why" questions directed to God about the problem itself. And then, people often start to think through all the ramifications of how their lives will change in the future. In the end, there will be a pretty significant dose of *fear*—fear of the pain; fear of the prognosis; fear of how others will respond; fear of the suffering itself; and possibly even fear of death. Anyone suffering from a disease, disability, or disorder will have to face the fear that comes along with the problem. But there is a much more "silent fear" that amasses around the sufferer—one that typically comes only in whispers in the congregation: the fear of how to relate to someone in the midst of suffering.

FEARING DISEASE

One of your deacons has been diagnosed with a brain tumor. The entire church rallies around him with great faith and sacrificial service. But then one of the teenagers in the youth group develops a rare form of cancer. Within just a few short months, a victim of stroke, a member with an undiagnosed genetic disease, and a child with a birth defect all hit the prayer chain. Why is all this happening to us? It seems, to many, like a satanic attack. So, the fears build. Even though our rational minds say that these diseases belong to individuals and are not a part of some sort of group virus, our fears say otherwise. What if

I'm next? How would I handle being struck by cancer? While we may not show that fear to fellow congregants, it can manifest by unthinking avoidance, which becomes interpreted by sufferers as a lack of love. That's what fear typically does—it protects self by avoiding whatever provokes the fear.

So, even though Christians do not have to fear death any longer, many still may have a fear of the prospect and process of death. In other words, the pain that goes along with disease can become most terrifying. Combine this with the fear of rarely getting much relief in this life, and it can be overwhelming. Now, think of what this fear promotes in the life of the congregation. Connecting fear of the disease as a lack of faith in God, church members can miss seeing the sufferer and just see the sinner. Certainly, we want those who have a severe illness or disease to grow in their faith in God, but what if fellow believers are attempting to motivate that growth by fear? Our fear of people not responding well to their disease will only end up pulling us apart relationally. It's hard to comfort someone who is suffering with a disease when you are afraid of how that person will handle it.

FEARING DISABILITY

What is there to fear about someone with a disability who begins to attend your church? First, it often presents us with the unknown. How do I communicate with this individual? What help does he or she need in order to be included in worship, Sunday school, or the other ministries of the church? Will I say or do something dumb or insensitive? Michael Beates frames the problem in this way:

> *Disability ministry demands a church willing to risk the unknown, to break down barriers, and to enter into the experiences of people and families who live with disability. It demands imagination and creativity, a willingness to make mistakes and learn along the way, but most of all, it demands taking the risk of being available and having people with disabilities present among the fellowship.*[18]

This fear of the risk involved is certainly legitimate, but it must not be allowed to be such an overwhelming barrier that it keeps us from entering into the suffering of others. Instead of fearing the making of a mistake, we must learn from our mistakes without avoiding people touched by disability.

Another potential fear that our congregations experience concerning disability is that the need is just too great. A widow who is bound to a wheelchair loves coming to her seniors' Sunday school class, but her caretaker isn't available to drive her to church and back home every Sunday. So her daughter, who goes to another church, asks the deacons if they can provide transportation, including getting her in and out of the vehicle. While diaconal hearts certainly want to show this compassion, the fears build as the week-to-week grind occurs. How can we sustain this level of help when we need to get our own families to church? Certainly, it requires wisdom to find a solution, but underlying fear can cause them to simply quit on this widow with a disability. As Beates says, being available to people with disabilities brings risk—and we have to calm our fears in order to move toward such people, and not away.

FEARING DISORDER

Consider this observation: "We can talk about diabetes and Aunt Mable's lumbago in church—those are seen as medical conditions . . . but mental illness—that's somehow seen as a lack of faith."[19] While it may be somewhat of an overstatement that most congregants consider mental and emotional disorders to be simply a lack of faith, this researcher is clearly picking up on a fairly typical problem in many churches. Simply put, there is a certain amount of fear in the local church about mental and emotional disorders. There can easily be fear in the hearts of the ones struggling with a disorder: fear of being rejected, fear of being stigmatized, and fear of being judged. As we will discuss further, when a church exudes an attitude that Christians "have it all together," then it only increases the fear of revealing the struggles the person is experiencing. I hear in my biblical counseling office all the time questions like this: "Dr. Kwasny, is this the worst problem you have ever heard?"

Isn't there also the reality that there is fear in the hearts of those who aren't currently struggling with some sort of disorder? Again, we can be afraid of the unknown. But what is there to fear when, in confidence, someone shares with you that he's struggling with depression and suicidal thoughts? What about a member in the youth group who thinks he is transgendered? Or the college girl who confesses she is anorexic? These are frightening problems, aren't they? They will provoke fear when we are unsure that real change can happen. They will also create a fearful response when we don't know what to say or do. So, it becomes easier to ignore mental and emotional problems, or just write them off as private, personal problems. Fear will keep our mouths shut out and our hearts closed to the real needs that are sitting right beside us. We will also fear being "real" to one another.

OVERCOMING FEAR WITH LOVE

Thankfully, there is a biblical solution to the fear that suffering can bring into a congregation. While an increase of fear can equate to a lack of faith in the power of God, it is also connected to diminished love. As the apostle John states: "There is no fear in love, but perfect love casts out fear. For fear has to do with punishment, and whoever fears has not been perfected in love" (1 John 4:18). Do you see how love is the opposite of fear? Fear builds walls; love tears them down. Fear pulls back; love enters in. Fear protects self; love sacrifices for others. In order to face our normal, human fears of disease, disability, and disorder, we must be growing in our love for Christ and our love for one another. No, we will never be perfected in love in this lifetime; sinful fears will always crop up in church life. But we can face our fears by enjoying the perfect love of Christ ourselves, and sharing that same love to all who suffer in our midst.

CONFRONTING OUR IDOLS

What is an idol of the heart? According to Timothy Keller, it is "something besides Jesus Christ that we feel we must have to be happy, something that is more important to our heart than God, something that is enslaving our heart through inordinate desires."[20] It is pretty easy to recognize the "headlining" sorts of idols in our world: power, fame, sex, money, etc. But what sorts of idols are ruling our hearts when it comes to the suffering occurring in our churches? In our week-to-week worship and ministry among one another, what are things besides Jesus Christ that we feel we *must have* to be happy? Unfortunately, even as Christians, we can idolize the same sort of things our world idolizes. And these idols prevent us from the loving pursuit of sufferers.

An image idol

You may think that this first idol only occurs in churches that are populated mainly by the upper class with "white collar" sorts of jobs. Or, more likely, it's just more obvious in those settings. Following the pattern of this world, we can idolize the perfect, the fit, the healthy, and the beautiful. Just like what is often shown in our social media feeds, it's tempting to portray the image of "no problems here" in our church. After all, we want other people to see only our best side, right? By definition, this idol is as surface-oriented as it gets. Writing about disability and the church, Jeff McNair reminds us: "People with disabilities are not an example of imperfection to the perfect. They are examples of imperfection to the imperfect who think they are perfect."[21] Deep down, Christians know they aren't perfect. Yet the entrance of disability, disease, and our disorder can certainly make us fight for the image of perfection. The problem comes when our love for sufferers is deterred by our love for only what the world defines as beautiful or attractive. Unfortunately, we can too often think that all that is unhealthy, unfit, and disordered is ugly.

I was once told the story of a major evangelical church that intentionally displayed to the world an idol of image. Because their worship service was nationally televised, it was important to them that only the good-looking, well-dressed members were seated in sections where the cameras were focused. This church policy meant that, not only were the poorer members of the church relegated further back in the sanctuary, but also those confined to walkers and wheelchairs. In other words, the church was to be seen by the world as healthy, happy, and wealthy. Hopefully, this is an extreme example that rarely happens in Christ-honoring churches. Yet, on an individual level, it can certainly be tempting to push those who are suffering to the sides and the edges of the congregation—or at least to the periphery of our own vision. It is just so much easier to be attracted to the "attractive," isn't it?

A COMFORT IDOL

While there is absolutely nothing godly or righteous about being focused only on image, the idol of comfort is actually a distortion of something good. Writing to the church at Corinth, Paul proclaims:

> *Blessed be the God and Father of our Lord Jesus Christ, the Father of mercies and God of all comfort, who comforts us in all our affliction, so that we may be able to comfort those who are in any affliction, with the comfort with which we ourselves are comforted by God.*
>
> *(2 Corinthians 2:3-4)*

As people who are given incredible comfort by God, Christians are to be always passing on that comfort to others who are suffering. As Paul says, we are *able* to comfort others with the same comfort that God has given to us! So, people struggling with disease, disability, or disorder should be able to count on believers as a source of their comfort.

Yet, instead of passing on comfort, we can often indulge in the comfort of God as an end in itself. And what does that produce? Comfortableness! It makes comfort our idol instead of the expression of our love for God and other people. Add to this the fact that people who are suffering tend to make us *uncomfortable*, which is no fault of their own. Thus, our idol of being comfortable is exposed when there are people with afflictions around us. We see their discomfort and cling to our own comfort. Sure, we may help a little, but don't push us too far out of our comfort zone! Just go to a church respite care facility for people touched by disability and see how it elucidates your idol of comfort. For me, all I need to do is spend a few hours in the hospital and I tend to become very uncomfortable. Instead of focusing on how to comfort others with the comfort of a comforting God, we hog God's comfort for ourselves. Or worse, we seek our comfort outside of God, with things that only bring temporary comfort.

A CONTROL IDOL

Some of us have a deep need for certainty—the need to know how absolutely everything is going to work out. That certainly sounds oxymoronic for Christians who believe that God is in control of all things! Yet this idol can be present itself even if we know that God is sovereign. It emerges from a desire to be as powerful as God, being able to find peace inside ourselves instead of in our dependence on him alone. This idol is exposed in our hearts when times of uncertainty come—when we aren't sure how things are going to work out. Thus, anxiety and fear build while we try to get our lives back under control. Any sort of suffering in our lives can certainly cause us to grasp for our idol of control!

How do we recognize this idol in the church? For example, there's a boy in your third-grade Sunday school class who has been diagnosed with ADHD. You quip to another parent: "I'm not buying it. If his parents would just be better disciplinarians, this problem would easily go away." Or, how about this one: A woman with quadriplegia needs someone to hold her bulletin, Bible, and hymnbook. One church member says to another, "I'd help her, if she wasn't so demanding all the time." And finally: A youth is struggling with same-sex attraction. When some parents hear of it, they start to gossip about how this teen should not be allowed in the youth group. Do you recognize the idol of control here? It often manifests when we think we have all the answers for the suffering of another. We are more interested in selling a quick fix without working toward any true understanding of the person, or the problem itself. And if it can't be fixed, we would rather have it removed from our field of view. Instead of entering in to the suffering of another, we want to control it, eradicate it, and explain it away. The control we want in our own lives leaks into how we treat (and thereby control) other people.

OVERCOMING IDOLATRY WITH RIGHT WORSHIP

A Christlike love will overcome our fears of those who are suffering in our midst. But heart idols will only be slayed when we work to change the focus of our delight. As Keller rightly asserts: "Jesus must become more beautiful to your imagination and more attractive to your heart than your idols. That is what will replace your counterfeit god."[22] To kill our idol of image, we see the image of God in *all* people who are suffering in our midst. To defeat our idol of comfort, we praise the God of all comfort and worship him alone. To overcome the idol of control, we marvel at the work of God in the lives of others, trusting in his power alone. The right worship of God puts God at the very center of the suffering of people, not off to the periphery. It is engaged with what God is doing in our church and among his people, not what we ourselves are doing. Jesus must become more beautiful to us than our need for all things to be "right" in our lives, and in our church!

DEALING WITH DISTRACTIONS

If modern people know anything at all, we know distractions! A distraction, of course, is anything that prevents someone from giving full attention to something else. Crying babies can certainly be a distraction in the worship service. Typically, when an infant is inconsolable, most parents remove that distraction (what a sad way to refer to sweet baby, right?) from the sanctuary. Then there are those people who advocate for children's church based on the belief that children are a distraction to worshiping adults. And, most recently, there are all those technology distractions—cell phones, tablets, etc.—that can keep us from giving full attention to the worship of God. So, what happens when it is a person with a disability, disease, or disorder who is deemed to be a distraction in the various events of church life? What do we do about this potential problem that suffering creates?

DISTRACTIONS IN WORSHIP

Matt, a twelve-year-old boy with autism, claps his hands three times every five minutes or so during the worship service. Matt's parents are actually impressed that he can sit through the entire service without trying to stand up and leave. Yet, the people sitting around this new family in your church are having trouble focusing on the sermon. Even the pastor has commented that the young man is being far too distracting, disturbing his concentration as well. The obvious solution is to remove Matt from worship. Yet, this raises important questions. Where else will he hear the Word of God preached? How will the family respond to the assertion that their child is a distraction? And, how much distraction is too much for other worshipers? This is certainly a different sort of problem than simply seeking to slay our heart idols. The needs of the many are clashing with the needs of the few. This is the distracting nature of suffering. It calls us to pay attention to it, and seek to do something about it.

Let's look at this obstacle from the perspective of a sufferer, with another example. Julie lost her mother to cancer six months ago. Her grief has led to panic attacks, especially when she is sitting in the worship service. She has learned to quietly slip out when the anxiety begins to build, but she feels likes everyone is watching her. Maybe it would be better for her to just not come to church for a few months. So, how would you counsel your good friend Julie in this situation? Or here's a better question: How could you walk alongside her during this difficult struggle? Hopefully, Julie's quick-fix solution isn't motivated by simply not wanting to distract other people, but it probably is. We need Julie to know that she has a church full of brothers and sisters in Christ who want her to be able to worship God in the midst of his people!

DISTRACTIONS IN LEARNING

Gus, an older gentleman with schizophrenia, has been coming to the adult Sunday school you teach regularly. Most of the time, Gus sits in the back row and doesn't say a word. But when you make some time for class discussion, he can blurt out some rather inappropriate things. Distracting, right? While it is understandable for church members to think he is just mentally ill and wonder why he isn't in an institution, the bigger question is: For what purpose does God have him here in our church? He certainly is suffering with a disabling disorder, but he also appears to want to be a part of the body of Christ. What do you do with those two facts? And, what if Gus distracts the rest of the class from being able to learn effectively? Or, is this an opportunity to enfold someone into the class who needs to belong to a family?

Gigi, a fourth-grade girl with Down Syndrome, is struggling to sit through an entire catechism class on Wednesday nights at your church. Most evenings Gigi tends to want to pace in the back of the class, putting her hands over her ears if it gets too loud. Gigi's parents really want her to learn more about God and basic Christian theology. They also want her to be around other children her own age. So, in their minds a segregated class for special needs is out of the question. But other parents are complaining to you that their children can't learn in this distracting environment. Even the teacher is having difficulty. Again, the "easy" solution is (citing educational needs) to separate Gigi from the rest of her peers. Maybe she would learn better in a personalized environment. But what if the greater need is for relationships? Can the rest of the class learn to live (and to learn) with these distractions?

DISTRACTIONS IN RELATIONSHIPS

Bill is well known for being the town drunk. He cleans himself up just enough to make it to church on Christmas and Easter, but not too many other Sundays each year. His wife, Judy, and three sons, on the other hand, are faithful members, and they are at church every time the doors are open. From one vantage point, they are some of your core members, helping out in all sorts of ministries. Yet, Judy is regularly shunned by most of the rest of the women in the congregation because they think she is foolish for sticking with Bill. The boys are also regularly treated to whispers from their friends, especially when Bill ends up in detox, or a treatment center. How can parents allow their children to play with these boys, with the risk of an alcoholic father showing up? The harsh reality is that this is a distracting church family. How are church members supposed to relate to this family?

Then there's Pamela, who is well known for claiming to have a new problem every month. Sure, she's had some legitimate diseases through the years, but the gossip is that she is really just a hypochondriac. Unfortunately, it appears that the main congregational method of dealing with Pam is avoidance. The few people who have befriended her have reported that it was like dealing with a drowning person who just keeps pulling you underwater. Even the pastor has told his wife to steer clear of Pam and her "many disorders." Have the elders and/or the pastoral staff actually discussed how to best help Pam, as well as the congregation in this matter? Or has the unwillingness to address the situation just led to church gossip and the lack of true relational problem-solving? Since the church is to be all about Christian relationships, these "distractions" can lead us in a different direction from Scripture.

OVERCOMING DISTRACTIONS WITH WISDOM

A ringing cell phone during the worship serviced is easily solved by being disciplined enough to silence it. A misbehaving baby can be brought to the foyer or a "cry room." But the distractions brought to bear in church life by people who are suffering with disease, disability, or disorder are not so simple. Just conceiving of hurting people as distractions should make all lovers of God uncomfortable! Yet, if we don't address the issue of the sufferers that do bring real distraction with their suffering, then we will be reduced to unbiblical options—gossip, separation, and even outright rejection. Godly wisdom is required to handle each unique situation. These challenges demand that we enter fully into personal relationships to consider the various competing needs of everyone involved. To avoid these conversations and decisions will keep us from functioning as the healthy body of Christ.

FACING OUR APATHY

In his essays on life after World War II, John Dos Passos made this cultural observation: "Apathy is one of the characteristic responses of any living organism when it is subjected to stimuli too intense or too complicated to cope with."[23] This is exactly what can happen to us in the presence of too much human suffering. Most problems can certainly seem overwhelming and too complicated to cope with, at first. So instead of facing the suffering and entering into a relationship with the sufferer, we can become numb to it, avoid it, and pretend it doesn't exist. The very essence of apathy is the lack of passion for or interest in what *should* be moving or even exciting. Thus, a great barrier to connecting disease, disability, and disorder to the church is the presence of an apathetic heart. It approaches suffering with a lack of emotion that should not characterize the believer. How, then, does apathy develop in the church among people who should be passionately loving others with the love of Christ?

MEANINGLESSNESS

The shortest route to apathy is to look around our world and perceive no real purpose. The question "Why do bad things happen to good people?" has led many people to conclude that

God doesn't exist, God is not all-powerful, or God isn't love. When suffering in our churches seems too frequent and too widespread, it's tempting for people to see little meaning in it all. On the outside, people in the pew may talk about God being in control, and all things being designed for a purpose; but, their faith may be struggling mightily on the inside. Like the Preacher writes, "In my vain life I have seen everything. There is a righteous man who perishes in his righteousness, and there is a wicked man who prolongs his life in his evildoing" (Ecclesiastes 7:15). When fine, upstanding Christian people develop life-threatening diseases, or have to live with chronic disability, where is the sense in it all? If I can't make sense of it, then it is easier to become numb to it.

HARDHEARTEDNESS

Apathy also develops in our hearts when our hearts have been hardened by sin. Time and time again, the Scriptures warn against developing a hardened heart against God, his commands, and the plight of people (Psalm 17:10, Matthew 19:8, 1 John 3:17). Suffering people around us can easily be ignored when our hearts are hardened by anger, bitterness, pride, and a myriad of other self-centered sins. When our hearts are not soft toward God, we will lack any warmth for the people that God has put into our lives. When our hearts are hard, suffering will not invoke much compassion. While this is clearly contrary to what a true lover of Jesus Christ is supposed to look like, it is too often present among our church members. Understanding this problem, James challenged the people of God this way: "If a brother or sister is poorly clothed and lacking in daily food, and one of you says to them, 'Go in peace, be warmed and filled,' without giving them the things needed for the body, what good is that?" (James 2:15-16). A hard heart will dismiss the sufferer without little emotion and ineffectual care.

FALSE GUILT

A final way apathy manifests in our hearts is when we begin to feel guilty for not helping people enough. If we are really paying attention to the needs that are all around us, it is easy to condemn ourselves for not doing more to meet those needs. "I should have cooked a meal for them after that long stay in hospital." "I should have spoken to that woman in a wheelchair, who always seems to be sitting by herself." The list of "shoulds" can become very long, producing a false sense of guilt. So a tempting solution to false guilt is apathy: "If I don't care, then I won't have to "do." Then, if I don't end up "doing," I won't feel bad about it. After all, I have enough to handle in my own life right now!" The truth is that it takes the entire church to meet the needs of sufferers at any point of congregational life. But the more people there are who "feel guilty" for not doing enough, even less will be accomplished.

OVERCOMING APATHY WITH EMPATHY

"When he saw the crowds, he had compassion for them, because they were harassed and helpless, like sheep without a shepherd" (Matthew 9:36). While apathy is a product of our sinful nature, empathy is the fruit of our being renewed in the image of Christ. Apathy moves away; empathy moves toward. Apathy refuses to feel; empathy feels deeply. Sometimes it's taught that empathy can only be given when you have actually "walked in someone's shoes." While it is true that having experienced a trial similar to someone else gives us opportunity for greater understanding, it is not the only source of empathy. Biblical empathy can be given to any person with any sort of suffering when we see people as Christ sees them. He saw them as harassed and helpless, sheep without a shepherd. Apathy doesn't see people at all—or sees them in unbiblical ways. Empathy sees people how they really are: people in need of a Savior, in need of redemption, in need of restoration! Christians feel deeply for people because of the love of Christ growing deeply in our hearts.

ADMITTING OUR INABILITY

Unless you are a trained and skilled helper of people, you probably think that someone else can help sufferers much better than you. Diseases, disabilities, and disorders certainly demand certain knowledge and expertise levels in day-to-day care. But our natural inclination to "leave it to the professionals" can wrongly cause us to altogether avoid people in the church who are suffering! As Brad Hambrick, writing about mental and emotional disorders, points out:

We often fail to realize that no professional qualifications are required to be a friend. As Amy Simpson in Troubled Minds wrote, "When churches have antibiotic-like expectations for mental health treatment, they communicate, 'go get treated, then you can come back and you can be a growing Christian with us.'" [24]

So, we must first understand that our inability must not keep us from caring for those who are suffering in our congregation. Then our inability will not just end in passivity, but move forward in Spirit-led activity.

WHEN WE FEEL HELPLESS

There are so many places in church life where we feel competent to help. Sign up to work in the nursery? Check. Help out on the church beautification work day? No problem. Teach a Sunday school class? Sure. Visit the sick? Maybe. Volunteer to be a buddy for a child with autism? Please find someone else. Complicated suffering has a way of bringing out our helplessness. It makes us see our own neediness first. And we would much rather do something—anything—that draws on our strengths instead of displaying our weaknesses. We think our inability disqualifies us from helping others in the church, but it is actually quite the opposite. As Welch points out, "Your neediness qualifies you to help others. Your neediness, offered well to someone else, can even be one of the greatest gifts you give to your church." [25] And, in the words of Paul: "But he said to me, 'My grace is sufficient for you, for my power is made perfect in weakness.' Therefore I will boast all the more gladly of my weaknesses, so that the power of Christ may rest upon me" (2 Corinthians 12:9). It is precisely when we feel most helpless that we are ready to help in many essential ways!

WHEN IT'S EXHAUSTING

But we know that serving people who are suffering is extremely tiring, right? If you have any doubts, just ask a caretaker, a parent who has a child with a disability, a medical professional, or a counselor. Fatigue has a way of convincing us that we are unable to help. In our service to those around us, we can easily become physically, emotionally, mentally, and spiritually tired. Yet again, we have encouragement to persevere in our exhaustion by God's Word. Listen to the apostle Paul:

> *And let us not grow weary of doing good, for in due season we will reap, if we do not give up. So then, as we have opportunity, let us do good to everyone, and especially to those who are of the household of faith. (Galatians 6:9-10)*

Doing good for others who are suffering will tempt us to give up at some point. To overcome this feeling of inability, we clearly need times of rest ourselves. Yet it is essential we recognize that our priority as the church is to become somewhat exhausted in order to help those full-time caretakers who are routinely well beyond utter exhaustion!

WHEN WE DON'T UNDERSTAND

Even with our advances in technology, there are so many things we still don't know about disease, disability, and disorder. We should be thankful when God grants understanding to people about any particular problem that humans experience! Typically, we tend to become very motivated to learn about the issues with which our closest family and friends have been diagnosed. So why do we allow our lack of knowledge to be a barrier to helping one another in the church? When a fellow church member describes the disease, disability, or disorder, why are we not seeking to learn more about it? We certainly have plenty of resources, literally at our fingertips! Granted, it takes work to weed through what is true and false; what fits within a biblical worldview of the person and what falls outside of it. Yet, as Christians we should never just simply throw up our hands and claim that the person's problem is beyond our understanding. We may not be gifted and skilled to give "professional" help, but a growing amount of knowledge increases our compassion, care, and concern!

WHEN WE ARE SUFFERING OURSELVES

Paul Tripp succinctly states: "You are a sufferer who has been called by God to minister to others in pain."[26] While it is true that our own suffering enables us to empathize and to be an encouragement to others, what if it actually becomes an obstacle to caring? When our own suffering is currently front and center in our lives, how can we actually be of help to others? Don't I need my suffering to be in the rearview mirror before I can turn my attention elsewhere? There is certainly a time where we are more in the place of receiving care than giving it. And sometimes there is just pure survival mode. But if we think that the church is filled with some sufferers and the rest of us who are always helping sufferers, this severely limits the body's work with one another. It will be a great barrier to congregational care if people who are suffering are not also in the mix of helping others who are suffering. We do all share suffering in common!

By definition, it is always a problem when disorders, disabilities, and diseases enter into the life of the church. But as an anonymous thinker once brilliantly quipped, "It is not what disease the patient has but which patient has the disease." Our churches are not filled with problems because of sin, sickness, and suffering—we are simply filled with people made in the image of God. Understanding the prevalence of our suffering, the problem of our suffering must necessarily lead us to further action. We must not let these obstacles keep us from our calling as the church, in its full three-dimensional fullness. As Joni Eareckson Tada writes: "Somehow we need Christians who will push through crowds, scale walls, and rip up roofs with that same urgent yearning to meet an ordinary need."[27] All of the 3-Ds of suffering certainly are ordinary in the sense that they are part and parcel of daily life. So, this passionate pursuing activity which must take place in the body of Christ is where we will turn our attention next.

For Personal Reflection

1. Think about the ways that the suffering of the people around you have personally impacted you. Honestly assess how their suffering has created a problem in your life, even if you do not consider the person(s) to be a problem in your life! (Note: In this sense, a problem is something that needs to be faced and dealt with, not just something that is painful.)

2. Reflect on the fears that keep you from entering into another person's suffering. What makes it difficult to move from fear to love?

3. The suffering of others has a way of exposing our heart idols of image, comfort, and control. Confess the idol that is most tempting to bow down to, and the hardest to destroy.

4. A common problem we have with suffering is that it distracts us from the things we would rather be doing. Think about the real distractions sufferers in your life present to you. Seek wisdom for how to overcome those distractions with patience and kindness.

5. As hard as it is to admit to being apathetic to certain suffering that is going on around you, the very nature of suffering can provoke it. Reflect on what types of suffering, as well as what sorts of sufferers, require more empathy from you instead of apathy.

6. Think about which of the 3-Ds of suffering you are most unable to handle in the people around you. Diseases? Disabilities? Disorders? Does your inability make you want to learn and grow more in it, or just avoid it?

For Church Assessment

1. Take an honest look at the members of your church: How comfortable are they with suffering and sufferers? This should not be an assessment rooted in harsh judgment or malice, but toward a goal of learning where your church needs to improve. Clearly, this assessment will be subjective and general, but it is important to know how your church is doing in seeing people who are willing to enter into suffering.

2. As a church, can members articulate their fears about suffering, or are they feeling under pressure to act like everything is just fine? If you are a church leader, what have you communicated to members about your own fears when it comes to diseases, disability, and disorder?

3. Assess your church for its general idols of image or comfort. How do your members handle individuals and families who visit your church? Think about how people who have some very noticeable suffering and who visit your church might view your congregation.

4. While no one wants to be labeled a "distraction," there are probably sufferers who distract others in the worship service, Sunday school, and other programs of the church. Rather than just wishing the distracting behavior would cease, think about ways to deal wisely and patiently with it. Church members may be complaining about the distractions—or they may even be impacting your ministry and worship. Don't avoid conversations about how to effectively address the distractions of suffering.

5. How best can we deal with the apathy of church members, as that is a very personal issue of the heart? Seek ways to proactively teach and preach empathy for all.

6. If there is gospel preaching going on in your church, then church members should be able to see and admit their inability. The tougher task is to not just give in to inability, thus allowing us to avoid hard things. Encourage people to get involved in places that push beyond their natural skills, personalities, or interests.

FOR GROUP DISCUSSION

1. Do people who are suffering expect too much from the church? Or too little?

2. What are the basic fears Christians can experience when it comes to helping people with diseases, disabilities, and disorders?

3. What heart idols does suffering expose in us as believers?

4. What specific ways does suffering create distractions in our lives and in our churches?

5. Overall, what do you think most people's attitudes are when they face the suffering of disease, disability or disorder? Do they tend toward apathy or empathy?

6. What sorts of suffering causes us to experience our inability the most? What are we to do about our inability in ministry?

7. What are the most difficult obstacles Christians face when it comes to members in our congregations who are suffering?

CHAPTER 3

THE PURSUIT OF SUFFERERS

Welcoming All Who Suffer to the Church

A couple from India who had been visiting our church for almost six months asked my daughter a surprising question: "Is your church racist?" Since our church is in the state of Mississippi, she thought they were just making a general observation of how segregated most of our congregations still are. But their question emanated from their own personal experience of not feeling welcomed. "We have been coming to your church for months and no one speaks to us. Do you not accept people from India?" Well that's a much different question! While we may have individual church members who are somewhat racist in their attitudes, a related problem is that we may just not be that welcoming to visitors who are different than "us." We are certainly warm to one another, and very friendly personally, but that doesn't always add up to being a welcoming church. And, unfortunately, a lack of feeling welcomed is often interpreted as a level of "hatred" towards people who appear not to be like us.

Let's change the scenario a bit. A person with longstanding depression visits your church and has very few people speak to him for over a year. "Does your church hate depressed people?" he asks. A woman with cerebral palsy sits alone with her husband week after week. "Is your church biased against people with who have CP?" A family with a young child with Down Syndrome attends for weeks without anyone saying more than a casual hello. "Does your church reject people with special needs?" It's one thing to "allow" people of all shapes and sizes to worship with you; it's wholly another to welcome them into the life of the church. This is the higher goal that the apostle Paul writes of to the church at Rome:

*May the God of endurance and encouragement
grant you to live in such harmony with one
another, in accord with Christ Jesus, that
together you may with one voice glorify the God
and Father of our Lord Jesus Christ. Therefore
welcome one another as Christ has welcomed
you, for the glory of God.*

(Romans 15:5-7)

So, what are the elements of true welcoming all who suffer into the local church? What does it look like, practically and biblically speaking?

A CHURCH OF THE WEAK

Writing on the church and disability from the perspective of 1 Corinthians 12, Amos Yong states: "The church is constituted first and foremost of the weak, not the strong: people with disabilities are thus at the center rather than at the margins of what it means to be the people of God."[28] Is this a mindset that most in your congregation have when they think about your church? A church full of weak people? Isn't that just giving in to a culture of victimhood or promoting self-pity? No, it just recognizes the truth of God's Word. It is God's way for his people, as the apostle Paul describes: "But God chose what is foolish in the world to shame the wise; God chose what is weak in the world to shame the strong" (1 Corinthians 1:27). Seeing people who are weak physically, mentally, and emotionally in our midst should remind us of the weakness we all share as God's people. We are all weakened by our sin, by our flesh, in our minds, and in our hearts. On our own, we only bring weakness to the table.

To be clear, a "weak" church is not a defeated church made up of people in utter despair. Instead, let's remind ourselves again of what the apostle Paul says about weakness. This should be our church model:

*But he said to me, "My grace is sufficient for
you, for my power is made perfect in weakness."
Therefore I will boast all the more gladly of my*

weaknesses, so that the power of Christ may
rest upon me. For the sake of Christ, then, I am
content with weaknesses, insults, hardships,
persecutions, and calamities. For when I am
weak, then I am strong.

(2 Corinthians 12:9-10)

A church of the weak is a church enjoying the power of Christ resting upon it! It is one that is full of people who are not focused on their own ability to do God's kingdom work, but on the grace of Jesus Christ needed to do that work. It is a body of people who, like Paul, are content in weakness because it allows God's strength to be made manifest. This is the weak church that confounds the strongest in the world.

When we have a right theology of the church, people suffering with disease, disability, or disorder find themselves right at home. Their weaknesses are put on display to see Christ at work in their lives. Rather than the "strong" and "able" and "problem-free" people being the most important, there is always room for all who recognize themselves as weak and needing the Savior. What will define who is at the "core" of your church is not those who do not have any physical, mental, or emotional problems, but instead, those believers who are growing toward maturity in Jesus Christ and unity with God's people. The focus becomes how we can serve one another in our weakness, not on those who "can" and those who "can't." Becoming a church of the weak goes against our natural desire to never appear as anything less than strong. Yet, it is the only way for the church to magnify the power of God to this world.

DIVERSITY, YET COMMONALITY

For the last several years, the leadership of our church has been taking more seriously God's call for the church to be culturally diverse. We have become convinced that this is a scriptural injunction and not just some sort of modern, liberal, political crusade. So, we have made great efforts to become more educated and equipped in order to reach out to our community and see people of all ethnicities worship together. After all, even though we may be different culturally, or politically, or socially, or economically—all Christians have Jesus in common. It is our sin, our comfort, and often our traditions that prevent us from enjoying more cultural diversity in many of our American churches. Hopefully, we can be a testimony to a divided world that the only true unity we have is in Christ. Diverse people can find true common ground in the church.

So, what if we adopt that same attitude and impulse regarding people with diseases, disabilities, and disorders? It's just too easy to think of the suffering of others as something that makes "them" different than "us." Those five people have cancer, the rest of us do not. We have ten individuals that we serve in our disability ministry—the rest of us have ability. Some of our members have mental and emotional disorders that require counseling and treatment, and all others do not. Do you see how we think? When we treat people as diagnostic categories instead of just as people, they seem so different than us during times of suffering. Yes, it's certainly true that we do have differences. Raising a child with autism is definitely different than raising a child without a diagnosable disability. Battling obsessive-compulsive disorder does set someone apart from others who are not. How then can we think through this diversity-yet-commonality construct when it comes to human suffering?

WE SHARE OUR HUMANITY.

On the list of the many things that are very sad about disease, disability, and disorder is how they all tend to dehumanize us. A man with brain cancer can go from feeling physically strong, intelligent, and articulate to being almost unrecognizable in the space of just a few months. Intellectual disabilities can make the special-needs Bible study group at your church appear (to outsiders) as a group of people who are unable to carry on normal conversation. The more severe psychotic disorders like schizophrenia can tempt us to see someone as just "crazy" rather than as a hurting person. While not many of us will admit to seeing sufferers as something less than human, this thinking is pervasive among us. Therefore, the first place to renew our minds to truly see *all* who suffer with *any* of the 3-Ds as human beings, made in the image of God. This must be embraced in our hearts, not just in our heads. Again, our churches are made up of people, not problems! Starting with our common humanity also means we see the beauty in God's creation of mankind. While the world is only amazed with its own definition of "perfect" bodies and minds, God's people are to see God's unique design in all people. We are to look beyond the surface and look for what makes us truly human. People are not perfectly functioning machines. They are not marvels of modern technology. Christians acknowledge the whole person, body and soul, inside and out. To be clear, this does not mean that we celebrate the ravages of disease and disability, or bodies and minds that are not functioning well. While we long for cure and change, we don't somehow "become" human when all is well in our lives. So we are to see beauty in all people, even when they are suffering—and even when they look or behave differently than we do.

WE SHARE IN SUFFERING.

So, our church is not made up of humans and non-humans— only people who need a Savior. But what about dividing ourselves between sufferers and non-sufferers? While that distinction may be true at a single point in time, it is patently false that there are only some of us who suffer and others who do not. As Paul Tripp comments, "Suffering is not only the common ground of human relationships, but one of God's most useful workrooms."[29] There is not a person alive who has not suffered in some way at some point. All of our bodies fail to function at times. We all struggle in our minds and emotions as well. No one has ever had a relationship untainted by sin. We all have some knowledge of inability and limitation. Now, before you think I am minimizing disease, disability and disorder, read the next heading. The point is that, while there is a grand diversity in our forms of suffering, we all have suffering in common in this life.

WE DON'T MINIMIZE OUR DIFFERENCES.

It typically doesn't help someone who has had several major depressive episodes to say, "You know, I get depressed sometimes, too." A person who has spent most of his life in a wheelchair will not be comforted by the words, "I once had a broken leg, and it was a real struggle for me." *So while we all suffer in this life, we all don't have the exact same experiences of suffering in extent, duration, and difficulty.* There's a reason we talk about certain people in our congregations having "Joblike" suffering. Having a relationship with someone who has a long-term disability will show you how different his life is from yours. When your friend spends months or even years in radiation and chemotherapy, you learn your differences. Our commonality does not translate to equality. The church is filled with people who are in all different places in their suffering, with wide gaps in between.

The presence of people with disease, disability, and disorder recognizes our common experience as humans as well as our diversity. So, if we look around and see the relative absence of human suffering, maybe we are sending the wrong message— that the church is not really for people with serious problems. Speaking specifically of disability and the church, Beates writes:

> *The absence of people with disabilities in the church indicates that the church has not yet grasped deeply enough the essence of the gospel; and conversely, God's people have drunk too deeply from the well of cultural ideology with regard to wholeness and brokenness.*[30]

Couldn't we say the same about disease and disorder, too? The essence of the gospel is that we are all broken people due to the fall. No one is whole and perfect. We all suffer in various ways. So, to exclude those with the most serious of suffering, or to not offer care and help in the church, is missing out on diversity, as well as the gospel of grace in Christ.

WELCOMING, NOT JUST FIXING

A patient sits in the doctor's waiting room with a set of expectations—diagnosis, treatment, and, hopefully, a good prognosis. It would be strange for this sufferer to be welcomed into the doctor's office, but then the doctor makes absolutely no effort to treat the illness. The same would be awfully curious at the counselor's office. It's nice to be made welcome; but the counselee would probably never go back if the counselor was not interested in helping him to deal with his mental or emotional disorder. So how do people typically enter the "waiting room" of a new church? They are probably not looking to get help with a physiological issue. People with disabilities are not usually seeking for a church to provide them with physical therapy or pain medication management. People could be looking for counseling from a pastor or a biblical counselor on church staff, but they are not necessarily looking for counseling from the person sitting next to them in the pew. The point is that entering into church life usually isn't first about seeking for the church to fix the suffering at hand. There is something bigger that the church must initially provide—a place to belong as a member of God's redeemed people.

Now let's be abundantly clear here. As will be the subject of the second half of this book, the church is biblically responsible to provide specific and unique care and counseling for all who are suffering. We should seek to give aid, accessibility, and answers to problems. The church, as the bearer of God's Word and the gospel, is definitely the place of hope, spiritual healing, and change. Yet as individual church members, we are not pursuing sufferers well if our only aim is to fix their problems. This "savior" mentality may end up short-circuiting true ministry which occurs within biblical relationships. We will not be communicating that sufferers are welcomed *just as they are* if our focus is fixing—but only as "patients" or "problems" that need to be solved. Let's consider some specific activities that will demonstrate our desire to enfold people as a significant part of the community of God's people.

ENTER THE SUFFERING.

When your dearest friend drops by your home, wouldn't you invite him or her to sit down, stay awhile, and visit with you? It would send quite a different message if you kept your friend on the front stoop, made brief polite chitchat, thanked him or her for stopping by—never allowing your friend to enter your home. After reflecting on the experience, your friend will probably ask you if there is something wrong, or if there was some sort of offense between you. In response, you say, "What are you talking about? I thought we had a great visit! I was friendly and warm and sociable! What more do you want?" Hopefully you see the problem here. It's one thing to "visit" briefly with people. It's quite another thing to let them "enter" into your life, where they feel relaxed enough to stay awhile. If we are to truly enter into the suffering of others, we are to first allow them entrance into our lives and our hearts. Then they just may allow us into their lives too.

As much criticism that there is rightly leveled against the friends of Job throughout the entire book of Job, sometimes we forget that they actually started off pretty well. After hearing of Job's severe hardships, we read these words: "And they sat with him on the ground seven days and seven nights, and no one spoke a word to him, for they saw that his suffering was very great" (Job 2:13). Now, you may argue that they should have said *something* over the course of an entire week! Yet, we can also see a picture of friends entering into the suffering of Job. Their faces were probably despondent, and tears had to be flowing. If they were truly grieving over Job's pain and losses, then they were connecting with him emotionally. That's how we begin to welcome someone, rather than just fix him or her. We feel deeply for our suffering friend, acknowledging how heavy and difficult it is. Whether a church member is newly diagnosed with a disease, suffering with disability, or troubled with a disorder, we are first called to enter the suffering, if invited. As we let people into our lives, we are much more likely to be welcomed into the lives of others.

HEAR THE SUFFERING.
Think for a moment about a person in your congregation who has a disability. Do you know the actual diagnosis, the etiology of the problem, and the long-term prognosis? Have you ever asked to hear the life story of the person with the disability? Do you have an understanding of the limitations, as well as the abilities and gifts, of that person? If not, you have some listening to do! And I would guess that most members of your congregation do as well. The reality is that we tend to stand at a distance and just assume what is going on in the person's life. Sure, you know that Benjamin was born with Down Syndrome. But what does that mean? What has been the progression of his disability? How has it impacted Ben's family? What other problems have emerged because of it? People who are suffering need to tell the story of their suffering. And they need people to listen.

But the heading of this section reads "Hear the suffering," not "Hear the story." When we are just listening to a person's story, it becomes more tempting to move in quickly to try to fix the problem. Instead, as those who are loved by a God who hears our suffering, we are to listen to a person's heart in the matter. Let's return again to the book of Job for a biblical example. Right after Job's friends sit quietly for a week with their grieving friend, Job speaks in chapter 3. If you read the chapter, Job doesn't tell his story, but profoundly expresses his pain and suffering. The state of his heart is on display in a remarkably vulnerable way. But unfortunately, Job's friends don't give him nearly enough time to talk, or respond empathetically to what he shared. One by one, they quickly transform into critical, condemning counselors who assume, presume, and end up in deep sin themselves. We can end up following the same pattern if we don't really hear the heart of the sufferer. Even if we know some of the "facts" of the problem, we will end up missing the person.

*A*SK HOW TO HELP.

Let's return one more time to the book of Job. After Job shares his heart, here's how chapter 4 opens: "Then Eliphaz the Temanite answered and said: 'If one ventures a word with you, will you be impatient? Yet who can keep from speaking?'" (Job 4:1-2). Eliphaz and the other friends go on to lecture Job, telling him *why* he is suffering and *how* to solve it. Not one time do they stop and ask *how best to help*! Isn't that our temptation, too? We see someone who is displaying a certain set of symptoms, and we say: "You need to go see a doctor." We observe a friend with features of anxiety or depression, and we say, "You need to make an appointment with a counselor." While a friend may certainly need professional help, this is fixing first, rather than a focus on welcoming. Instead of telling someone what to do, it is so much better to *ask* how to help: "Wow, thanks for sharing your suffering with me. So, how can I help?" You will be amazed at the responsiveness you receive with these simple words. It communicates that the person is welcome into your life, in his or her present state, regardless of what care and help may be needed.

INVITING, NOT JUST WELCOMING

How about we go further than simply welcoming people with diseases, disabilities, and disorders into our congregations? What would that look like? Consider these challenging words from one church leader:

> *We've decided to quit being a welcoming church. No kidding. We're giving it up. Like so many congregations, we've sunk an amazing amount of time and energy into becoming a welcoming church. We changed worship styles, trained greeters and ushers, wore name tags, brewed coffee, went to workshops on hospitality and put our friendliest people in the most prominent places on Sunday mornings. My congregation realized that we had been misplacing our emphasis. Welcoming, from a missional perspective, is passive. It denotes waiting for visitors and guests to drop by. Inviting is different. Inviting is active. Being an inviting church means that we leave the comfort of Sunday morning worship and seek out our neighbors. Being an inviting church starts with who God has called us to be as church and mandates joining God at work in the world.*[31]

Seeking. Pursuing. Inviting. Moving from being passive to active. This sort of active engagement is a challenge for many of us when it just comes to people in our immediate neighborhood. So what about inviting a person you meet at the supermarket who has a pronounced disability? Or pursuing a neighbor who has told you she suffers from mental illness? It's one thing to invite people who we would enjoy worshiping alongside of to our church. How do you challenge yourself and your fellow church members to invite those who are suffering?

Jesus gets to the heart of the matter in Luke 14. He gives an important instruction after watching human nature—people giving the rich and famous the "places of honor."

> *He said also to the man who had invited him,*
> *"When you give a dinner or a banquet, do not*
> *invite your friends or your brothers or your*
> *relatives or rich neighbors, lest they also invite*

you in return and you be repaid. But when you
give a feast, invite the poor, the crippled, the
lame, the blind, and you will be blessed, because
they cannot repay you. For you will be repaid at
the resurrection of the just."

(Luke 14:12-14)

Now, we can certainly see the spiritual aspect of this command, recognizing that Jesus could be referring to all who are spiritually poor, crippled, lame, and blind. Yet, in context, this mandate is dealing with the fact that even Christians tend to only "invite" people into their fellowship who are rich, powerful, and healthy. Why is that? According to Jesus, it's because those sorts of people can "repay" us in some way. But the people who are suffering with disease, disability, or disorder do not have the same capacity to pay us back in the usual ways.

Let's push that picture deeper into our hearts. What does it mean to invite someone to dinner or a banquet? It's a uniquely special event. It's usually designed for the most intimate of relationships (family, friends, etc.). It's a joyful and festive celebration. It is always an honor to be invited to someone's banquet. This is not just descriptive of inviting people to our personal events, but pursuing them into the life of the church! We are to pursue people to celebrate the Lord Jesus together. We are to invite people to the most special of all events: the worship of God each and every week! We are to seek the sufferer out as the most desirable of people since such are marginalized by most of the rest of society. As Yong writes concerning disability and the church: "From a missional perspective, the church is charged not only with inviting people with disabilities into its community but also with bringing them in and honoring their contributions."[32]

This sort of inviting and welcoming is usually foreign to people who are suffering with disease, disability, or disorder. A person who has just recently had a stroke may have to adjust his lifestyle in such a way that he no longer attends the events and activities he once enjoyed. The testimony of a parent of a child with a disability is that her daughter never gets invited to a peer's birthday party or other special events. Many of the most common disorders, like anxiety, depression, and addictions can also keep people on the outside of the celebrations of life. A church that does more than tolerate—does even more than welcome—people who are suffering will be pleasantly surprising to many. "You really want me to be a part, even in my present state?" And the response should be: "Not just a part— you and your family are our special guests! We would be lost without you!"

Persevering for the Long Haul

It's often tempting to treat suffering as if it should always be temporary. A person who has lost a loved one is "allowed" to grieve for a little while, but not for too long. Illnesses should last just a short time, because people have to get back to work. We visit people regularly in the hospital at the beginning of a sickness, but tend to lose track of those in long-term facilities. Certainly, it is understandable that people desperately want healing to be quick, or significant change to be timely. Yet for many people who are suffering, this just isn't reality. Joni Eareckson Tada celebrated her fiftieth year in a wheelchair in 2017. There are probably people in your congregation who have been struggling with disease, disability, or disorder for years and even decades. As much as God has chosen for them to persevere in their suffering, they need others to endure with them as well.

The church of Jesus Christ is in the unique position to walk with sufferers for the long haul. It is the practical outworking of a relationship with Jesus Christ. Consider how the writer of Hebrews speaks of the Christian life:

> Therefore, since we are surrounded by so great
> a cloud of witnesses, let us also lay aside every
> weight, and sin which clings so closely, and let
> us run with endurance the race that is set before
> us, looking to Jesus, the founder and perfecter of
> our faith, who for the joy that was set before him
> endured the cross, despising the shame, and is
> seated at the right hand of the throne of God.
> (Hebrews 12:1-2)

Clearly, our sin slows us down in the endurance race that lies before us. But so can disease, disability, and disorder. These are things that so easily weigh people down. In those contexts, we call people to keep their eyes on Jesus in order to persevere. But we are also supposed to be those brothers and sisters in Christ who are running the Christian marathon right alongside of them! Without one another, we will find it much harder to reach that finish line, especially in the presence of any of the 3-Ds.

For many who are suffering under the burden of long-standing disease, disability, or disorder, people are regularly coming in and out of their lives. Medical professionals, counselors, and therapists are often short term in the process. Some friends may be in it for the long haul, yet other friendships are short-lived. While some family members will probably be around the longest, even those relationships can become strained or distant at times. Yet the church, even in all its imperfection, must always be there! We should be the consistently welcoming, pursuing, inviting place (and people) for all who suffer. In this way, the church of Jesus Christ is called to give people a picture of heaven, the end point of our perseverance. Only there, in our glorified bodies, before the High King of heaven, will we be without our suffering for eternity! We pursue sufferers with the commitment to run the race with them as long as we are able.

DISPLAYING THE HEART OF GOD

People who are suffering can develop all sorts of wrong views of God, depending what they are experiencing and how they have been taught. Some can come to believe that God always wants them healthy and happy, so their faith must be lacking. Others can think God is kind of impotent when it comes to certain suffering, blaming an all-powerful devil. But a nearly universal response to God, especially at the outset of suffering, is either: "Why me, God" or "God, where are you?" In other words, our pain and trials can often lead us to question if God loves us, if He really cares, or even if we are being punished for some sin. Because of these misperceptions of God, a great need for Christians in our midst who are suffering is to know the truth of the heart of God. They need to come to know a God who acts from a heart of compassion. As he saw the Israelites, he sees his people's suffering today: "Then the Lord said, 'I have surely seen the affliction of my people who are in Egypt and have heard their cry because of their taskmasters. I know their sufferings . . . .'" (Exodus 3:7).

So if a member of our church is struggling to see the goodness of God in her suffering, what is our role in it? Job's friends misrepresented God as simply a punisher of sin, declaring that Job must have been quite a secret sinner since he was suffering so much. Can we project a similar false image of our loving and gracious God by presuming we know *why* people are going through their tribulations? Now, please don't misunderstand. A right view of God includes his holy and righteous discipline for sin. If Job was being punished for his sins, then his friends would have had a correct perspective. The problem is that none of us knows exactly *why* a person is suffering or *what* God has planned for him or her. But what we do know is that God loves his people and has compassion on all their suffering—whether it is self-inflicted or others-inflicted. So, a big part of the church's task in helping others is reflecting the love of God from beginning to end.

In what sorts of situations is putting the heart of God on display required the most? Gail is a sixteen-year-old in your youth group. She began drinking as a fourteen-year-old, and now she has moved on to harder drugs. Recently, she has been sharing with her closest friend that she is regularly depressed. Does Gail need her peers in the youth group and other mature adults in her life to confront her sin and rebellion? Certainly! But is that all she needs? Yes, she is suffering partly due to her own choices. Yet, upon further investigation, you discover Gail has been raised by a very controlling mother and an emotionally absent father. Her "disordered" behavior needs change, but it also demands pursuit of a heart that is suffering. Gail needs to know a God who sees and knows her as both a sinner and a sufferer. While it may appear that we downplay sin when we put the love of God on display, it is quite the opposite. When Christians truly know God's love for them, they can become convicted by the Spirit and enjoy God's grace for change.

Let's try another one. Carl, a fifty-five-year-old man in your church suffers with quadriplegia and a severe visual impairment. At a men's retreat, you had a chance to hear his story for the first time. You knew Carl was in a car accident as a young man, but you didn't know it was his own fault—he was drag racing his sports car illegally. Does that piece of information change how you approach him as a friend? Sure, the person who suffers a lifetime of disability due to the sin of another deserves all of our love and compassion. But, what about Carl? Since he got what he "deserved," does that mean God doesn't love him—even as a professing Christian? As you enter into more of his suffering, that is exactly what he has struggled with the most—the notion of a God who, as a Father, loves him even in his own foolishness. Sure, if Carl hadn't yet confessed his sin and accepted the responsibility for his disability, you may have had conversations about those things. But instead, you can point Carl to the heart of God with these words of the psalmist: "Out of my distress I called on the Lord; the Lord answered me and set me free" (Psalm 118:5).

If we only put the love of God on display to people when they appear to be "innocent" in their suffering, then we don't truly understand the merciful heart of God. His love is not divorced from his holiness and justice. So, when we are in pursuit of sufferers as the church, we are to always show others the love of God as people who are first loved by God. This amazing love is expressed perfectly by the apostle Paul:

> But God, being rich in mercy, because of the great
> love with which he loved us, even when we were
> dead in our trespasses, made us alive together
> with Christ—by grace you have been saved. . . .
> (Ephesians 2:4-5)

The same love and grace of God unto salvation is at work in our sanctification. This is the love that welcomes suffering sinners to grow in grace. Every time we are pursuing those who are overburdened by sickness of body and soul, we are putting the love of God on display to a watching world.

IMITATING THE SUFFERING SERVANT

Isaiah 53 is the classic prophecy of Jesus Christ as the "Suffering Servant." What a way to describe King Jesus! It's exactly what people living in a fallen world need to have in a Savior—one who suffers with us and for us. As familiar as these words may be to you, consider them in light of pursuing sufferers into the church:

> *For he grew up before him like a young plant,*
> *and like a root out of dry ground; he had no*
> *form or majesty that we should look at him, and*
> *no beauty that we should desire him. He was*
> *despised and rejected by men, a man of sorrows*
> *and acquainted with grief; and as one from*
> *whom men hide their faces he was despised, and*
> *we esteemed him not. Surely he has borne our*
> *griefs and carried our sorrows; yet we esteemed*
> *him stricken, smitten by God, and afflicted. But*
> *he was pierced for our transgressions; he was*
> *crushed for our iniquities; upon him was the*
> *chastisement that brought us peace, and with his*
> *wounds we are healed.*
>
> *(Isaiah 53:2-5)*

How often do we think of Jesus this way? No beauty; despised and rejected by men; a man of sorrows and grief; one from whom men hide their faces; stricken; smitten; afflicted. These are words and phrases to which people with disease, disability, or disorder can certainly relate! No, Jesus didn't suffer with cancer, or a disability, or a mental or emotional disorder. And yet, he genuinely suffered as a human being, without sin, bearing the sins of his people.

People who are saved by the suffering and death of the Lord Jesus Christ are also called to a life of suffering for him. As the apostle Paul states succinctly: "For it has been granted to you that for the sake of Christ you should not only believe in him but also suffer for his sake. . . ." (Philippians 1:29). Tripp puts it this way: "Suffering is a sign that we are in the family of Christ and the army of the kingdom. We suffer because we carry his name. . . . We suffer so that we may be part of the good he does in the lives of others."[33] All of our suffering is certainly not due to the fact that we are carrying the name of Christ. But the fact that we do serve a suffering Savior means we are to imitate him by serving *in* our suffering. And that should mean that we pursue any sort of sufferer in order to ultimately point him or her to the Savior.

Why do we pursue people in whatever state of suffering they exist? The gospel gives us a simple answer: Because that's how Christ pursues us. He calls us in our brokenness and our inability. He puts us together as his body in our weakness. He brings together a wide diversity into a common community of faith. So we welcome, not just fix. We invite and pursue, not just welcome. We persevere and endure with one another. And how can we do all these impossible things? Only because of the grace of God, the work of Christ, and the power of the Spirit! Praise God that he first pursued us so that we can pursue others in Christ.

For Personal Reflection

1. Think about when you first visited your current church. Did you feel welcomed? If so, what were some tangible ways that you were welcomed?

2. Consider how you envision a "strong" Christian versus a "weak" Christian. How do you view yourself? If a strong Christian is one who most looks like Christ, how should that Christian also be weak?

3. Reflect on your personal beliefs about diversity. Is more diversity in your own personal sphere of relationships an active goal of yours? Having friends or acquaintances from a different cultural expression is a good thing. So, what about relationships with people who have different expressions of suffering?

4. While we all want to be welcomed when we enter into a new place or relationship, be honest about your own capacity or interest to welcome others. Is your life essentially closed to new relationships because you believe you have enough people in your life? What needs to happen to help you open your heart to people who are suffering?

5. Think about three people in your church who are struggling with a disease, disability, or disorder. Take time to ask to hear their stories. Listen to their various journeys through suffering. Thank them for the privilege of knowing their stories.

6. If you know that suffering is to be a central part of the Christian life (because we serve a suffering Savior), challenge your heart to embrace it. Consider whether you are resistant to enter another's suffering because it doesn't fit into your definition of the Christian life.

7. Think about how you are suffering right now—with disease, disability, disorder, or some combination of the three. Are you allowing others to suffer with you? Do you welcome people to enter into your suffering, or are you more interested in handling it yourself?

For Church Assessment

1. As you think about your congregation, would you say you have a church full of strong people, or weak people? Is the message that we only really want strong people who have it all together? Think about what a church "of" the weak and "for" the weak would look like.

2. Diversity in the church today tends to be code for having various ethnicities represented. While that is a good start, how diverse is your church when it comes to suffering? Are the disabled well represented? Do you have people with all sorts of disorders? While this line of questioning may make it appear that we actually desire for people to have all sorts of problems, it really just recognizes that people *do* have all sorts of problems. Where else would we rather have people with problems than as members of our churches!

3. Reflect on some of the practical ways your church welcomes people now and some of the ways it needs to grow in welcoming. Often, we think of just greeting people as they enter a worship service. Think more deeply about all the other more relational ministries of your church and how to make them more welcoming.

4. What are ways that church leadership inspires your church members to seek out the suffering in your community? Pursuing the suffering is a very personal activity, so think about how we are to stir one another up to good works. How are we doing that?

5. It's one thing to welcome people to our church; it's another to persevere with them. As you think about the people who have had chronic suffering in their lives, has the congregation lost track of them? How can church members become more engaged with people with long-standing suffering in their lives?

6. People in your church who are suffering with disease, disability, and disorder become weary of "being a burden," or always having a problem. Reflect on ways to communicate the welcoming message of bearing one another's burdens and sharing in the suffering together. How will they know those are more than mere words or clichés?

For Group Discussion

1. As you think about churches today, would you describe them as welcoming? Why or why not?

2. What does it mean to you to think of a local church as a "church of the weak"?

3. What is the state of diversity in most churches today? Have we intentionally thought of diversity extending to various types of sufferers?

4. What does it mean to welcome suffering people into your own life?

5. How do we change from just being welcoming, to pursuing people who are suffering?

6. What does it mean to persevere with someone who is suffering?

7. What does it mean to enter into someone's suffering?

THE CHURCH IN 3-D CARING FOR SUFFERERS

"... but that the members may have the same care for one another."

When we use the term "one-dimensional" in reference to a person, what do we mean? Typically, we are saying that the person is superficial and lacking in depth. So, what if your church is one-dimensional? How sad would it be for the gathered body of Christ to be considered as superficial, and without real depth to it all! Our Lord Jesus calls his people to much more—even though, by nature, we can tend to be one-dimensional. If we are going to truly deal with the 3-Ds of suffering, then more is required of us. Therefore, these last three chapters will focus on how the local church is to care for people with diseases, disabilities, and disorders.

Now, when considering the work of a particular congregation, we should begin by acknowledging that Christ has called his body to labor in manifold ways. Just because the underlying Greek word used most often for church (*ekklesia*) has as one of its meanings, "gathering," the church doesn't just get together to "hang out." While the local church is to be a close community, we are really to be more like a *task force*, gathered to accomplish the King's work in this world. This is especially true when it comes to dealing with diseases, disabilities, and disorders. The church is vital to the lives of people, and not just the ones who presume to be healthy! Following in the footsteps of the Great Physician, we work with all who are in need of spiritual, emotional, mental, and relational healing. Christians have responsibilities in the wider kingdom of God; but our priority is the work of the church. Therefore, we gather as the church in order to worship *and* to work.

When we acknowledge that there are jobs to be done as the church, we must take care not to succumb to a "felt-needs" approach to church life. In other words, the local church shouldn't choose what work to do primarily on the basis of what some or even most people perceive as need. Now, that doesn't mean we ignore the real needs of church members in some kind of unloving, insensitive way. We certainly seek to do works of service which will be of help to all who are in need. But believers must always do that work within the parameters of what God has called and equipped his church to be and do. So, just because our church members have cars that desperately need repair work doesn't necessarily mean that the local church should become an auto service center. *We look to the Word of God to keep us focused on all the vital responsibilities of the church.* And three main pictures of the church emerge: The church as a hospital, the church as a family; and the church as a disciple-making culture.

CHAPTER 4

THE CHURCH AS A HOSPITAL

Congregational Care in the Church

When moderns hear the word hospital, most of us immediately picture the multistoried concrete building where sick people receive medical care and are nursed back to health. So, to speak of the church as a hospital may conjure up images of sick beds in the hallways or the sanctuary as an operating room—right out of my favorite classic television show, *M*A*S*H*.[34] Or, the church-as-hospital notion may be wrongly thought of as putting forward a belief that Christians should view medical help as useless, with only faith and prayer as necessary for the diseased. While there certainly are a minority of professing believers in Christ who reject the entire field of medicine and believe the church is an actual substitute for the medical hospital, this is not a biblical understanding. We must recognize that God ordains and uses medical professionals, medical treatments, and medicine itself to restore health and offer pain relief to people with all sorts of diseases. Asserting that the church is a hospital for the diseased does not negate necessary medical help, but instead calls the church to an essential *hospitable responsibility* for those suffering in our midst.

The Picture of a Hospitable Church
HOST, HOSPITAL, HOSPITALITY, ETC.

The word *hospital* is rooted in the Latin word for "host," which is narrowly defined as a person who receives guests. So, the early use of hospital in both the Latin and the French was for a "guest house," or an "inn." That etymology alone demonstrates the vital connection between the correlated terms: "host," "hospital," "hospitality," and even "hostel" and "hospice." These host-based words give us the sense of providing care for important guests who need shelter and/or healing. Even when the word "hospital" began to be used more frequently in medieval England, it was descriptive of an institution which housed the needy.[35] Thus, our brief word study pictures for us a spectrum of everything that a "host" would do for another person: care for him, give him shelter, and make sure he's out of harm's way. The parable of the good Samaritan comes to mind when thinking of this etymology, as the Samaritan brought the wounded man to an inn where an innkeeper provided for his physical injuries (Luke 10:25-37). A hospital!

So while Christians individually are called to be hospitable people, the local church is called to be the most hospitable of all institutions. As Christine Pohl beautifully states: "Hospitality is at the heart of Christian life, drawing from God's grace and reflecting God's graciousness. In hospitality, we respond to the welcome that God has offered and replicate the welcome to the world."[36] The body of Christ is to always have a *host mentality*, embracing guests who are desperately looking for care and shelter. The church is called to be warm and friendly, engaging all who are looking for peace with God. For what does it say about Christ when Christians are cold, rejecting of visitors, and desiring to remain a closed, comfortable group? And what does the world think of Jesus when his followers are insensitive and unfeeling toward strangers and outsiders? The church is to be the greatest of all guest houses, a place of healing for all those who are outside of Christ—all who have sin-sick bodies and souls.

The writer of Hebrews gives us an intriguing motivation for practicing biblical hospitality as a church. In Hebrews 13:2, we read: "Do not neglect to show hospitality to strangers, for thereby some have entertained angels unawares." Wow! When we think we are just welcoming strangers into our midst, these folks could actually be angels in disguise? If this is true, how would this move the church to be more hospitable? For starters, we should remember the essential work of angels in Scripture. They are messengers from God. They encourage God's people. They protect and defend believers. With that understanding alone, why wouldn't we want angels in our midst? This makes the call of the church to be hospitable greater than just some sort of community social work for suffering people. The church is a hospital in order to glorify God *and* to enjoy the presence of his ministering and protecting angels. When it is tempting to *not* be hospitable because of the risk involved or the disturbance of our comfort, we should realize we have ultimate security in Christ from the angels of God!

A hospitable church is also to be a joyful church. Can you really have one without the other? The apostle Peter must have seen that as a possibility, so he gave this instruction: "Show hospitality to one another without grumbling." (1 Peter 4:9). The truth is that the regular work of hospitality can easily tempt us to complain and grumble, for a variety of understandable reasons. Most of all, hospitality can be exhausting! Or, as Pohl points out: "When we orient our lives around tasks, opportunities for hospitality often appear in the form of interruptions. When tasks completed become the measure of ministry, it is difficult to value relationships. . . ."[37] Therefore, we must guard our hearts and minds, working to show hospitality to all who are suffering, out of a heart of gratitude. This begins with church ministry leaders, as the apostle Paul reminds us about the main qualifications of elders: ". . . but hospitable, a lover of good, self-controlled, upright, holy, and discipline" (Titus 1:8). This leadership should then permeate the entire local church, driving us to the goal of joyful, relentless hospitality. The church will only be a hospital for the suffering when it lives up to the command to be hospitable (without grumbling) to all!

THE SPIRITUALLY SICK

An understanding of the church-as-hospital also pictures for us our need for the Great Physician. In the Gospel of Mark, Jesus says: "Those who are well have no need of a physician, but those who are sick. I came not to call the righteous, but sinners" (Mark 2:17). What was going on that Jesus needed to make this declaration? The scribes and the Pharisees had just accused our Savior of wrongly eating with tax collectors and sinners. After all, how can a ceremonially clean, Jewish teacher of the Law have fellowship with the unclean dregs of society? According to Jesus, he not only desires a social relationship with sinners, but came specifically to call sinners to be his disciples. And, by way of analogy, Christ declared that sinners are the spiritually sick; making him the Great Physician. So just as sick people need a medical doctor, all people need the healing work of Jesus!

Since Jesus is the Head of the Church (Colossians 1:18), that also makes him the Chief Administrator and Physician of his spiritual hospital, the local church. This hospital is to have its doors wide open to all who understand themselves to be sick sinners in need of spiritual health. Only those who see themselves as righteous outside of the work of the Great Physician are not welcome, as they are not called by Christ. And why would those "righteous" even want to be connected to the body of Christ? Just as the healthy would never seek a doctor or a hospital, the self-righteous in this life won't seek Jesus, or the hospitable community of believers. So the church is not first instituted for the physically diseased, but the spiritually sick. The church-as-hospital is for *all* sinners who are in desperate need of an eternal, spiritual cure.

Let's press the analogy a bit further. When sinners come to Christ, they are saved, forgiven, and cleansed from all unrighteousness. So, does that mean we only have a single "doctor's appointment" with the Great Physician and then we are permanently healed? While this certainly describes our one-time justification by faith alone in Christ alone, that doesn't end our need for healing. Christians need ongoing spiritual healing as we battle the ravages of sin and suffering in our lives. We require biblical change in all aspects of our lives—spiritually, mentally, emotionally, and relationally. This is the Spirit-led process of sanctification, where we not only visit the Great Physician on an occasional basis, but commune with him every day of our lives. Spiritual healing, then, is both a one-time salvific act as well as an ongoing work of growing into Christlikeness.

So, what does that ongoing work of sanctification have to do with the church-as-hospital? Maybe the M*A*S*H units of the Korean War is actually the best way to see the work of local churches. We are not just spiritually sick souls comfortably living out our days on earth in the church-as-hospital. No, Christians are in a spiritual war, living in bodies of sin, and suffering in a world of evil—with Satan as our chief enemy. By God's grace, the church is called and equipped to be a wartime hospital, offering gospel healing, comfort, and encouragement for all the suffering soldiers of Christ. As members of the body of Christ, we gather as the church to "bind up" our wounds, and "rehab" from the fight. Our sinful hearts impact us every day from the inside, and the devil and the world battle us on the outside. The Great Physician enlivens his church to be the welcoming spiritual hospital we all desperately need!

CONNECTING THE SPIRITUAL AND THE PHYSICAL

While Jesus was on earth, he was constantly faced with people who were sick and diseased. As his ministry progressed, the crowds only grew larger, apparently always including many who desired to be healed. Luke 4 describes a scene that was repeated over and over again during Jesus' ministry: "Now when the sun was setting, all those who had any who were sick with various diseases brought them to him, and he laid his hands on every one of them and healed them" (Luke 4:40). Jesus certainly could have declared that he was only on earth to save people from their sins. After all, what good is physical health if there is no spiritual health? But Jesus dealt with the entirety of human suffering, including physical diseases, affirming that human beings ae both body and soul, physical and spiritual.

Yet, when we read the Gospels, we should not see Jesus as primarily concerned with the physical health of people with diseases. All of his healings were more than just bringing relief of physical pain, even though that's a beautiful mercy. Jesus healed people physically to demonstrate that he also had the power and authority to heal people's sin-sick souls! This is illustrated for us in Luke 5, in the story of the paralyzed man who was lowered through the roof. We pick up the story in verse 20:

> And when he saw their faith, he said, "Man, your sins are forgiven you." And the scribes and the Pharisees began to question, saying, "Who is this who speaks blasphemies? Who can forgive sins but God alone?" When Jesus perceived their thoughts, he answered them, "Why do you question in your hearts? Which is easier, to say, 'Your sins are forgiven you,' or to say, 'Rise and walk'? But that you may know that the Son of Man has authority on earth to forgive sins"—he said to the man who was paralyzed—"I say to you, rise, pick up your bed and go home."
>
> (Luke 5:20-24)

Jesus' miraculous act of physical healing was a powerful demonstration of Jesus' main focus—the forgiveness of sin. The paralyzed man needed cleansing of sin much more than he needed physical health: Jesus was merciful to give him both sorts of healing. All of our diseases exist because we live in a fallen world, making the healing of our souls the main priority.

Christ's potent work of physical healing in order to illuminate our need for spiritual healing is a much-needed example for the church-as-hospital. It teaches us that our job of caring for sick and diseased people must never be separated from the rest of the gospel-driven work of his church. Another passage in the Gospel of Matthew assists us with this truth: "And he went throughout all Galilee, teaching in their synagogues and proclaiming the gospel of the kingdom and healing every disease and every affliction among the people" (Matthew 4:23). Jesus always connected his preaching of the gospel and his teaching of the Word of God with the practical healing of diseases and afflictions. The power of the gospel was shown to the people in life-giving Word and deed. So should it be in the church today. We preach and teach, proclaiming Christ to all who are spiritually diseased. We also minister to those who are physically sick through prayer, sacrificial giving, and mercy ministry. Seeing each person as a physical-spiritual entity allows the church to neither neglect preaching to the heart or caring for the sick body!

CONNECTING PHYSICAL NEEDS TO THE CHURCH

Picturing the church-as-hospital raises the question: Why do we need the church to be a hospital when we already have "real" hospitals? In other words, what business does the local church have in caring for the sick when we have medical professionals who are specially trained and skilled to do this important curative work? This question can reveal an underlying non-biblical bifurcation of body and soul, which views the place of "religion" for the soul and the work of medicine for the body. While people with diseases need medical help, this doesn't mean that medical assistance is *all* that is necessary. And, as was just demonstrated, we must keep in mind that the physical and spiritual dimensions of the human beings are always interconnected. Therefore, robust healing of the body must include the spiritual care that only Christ can give, often through the service of a hospitable church. Christians shouldn't only be limited to professional medical care when they are diseased, but also enjoy the congregational care of their local church.

One of the significant Scripture passages that clearly demonstrate this truth is found in James 5: "Is anyone among you sick? Let him call for the elders of the church . . ." (James 5:14). If all that is necessary when we are diseased is medical help, why do we need to call the elders of the church? As will be discussed later in this chapter, the elders are to pray over us for healing. This is just one of the essential practices of the local church for those who are diseased. Again, this activity is not to be seen as an alternative for medical help, but an important priority for the Christian and the church. Why wouldn't we seek the help of the Great Physician when we are diseased? Accordingly, why wouldn't we seek for believers, especially leaders of the church, to stand with us in prayer and petition for healing? This instruction by James was not just for ancient times, somehow rendered unnecessary with all our modern hospitals, technologies, and medicines. It's a clear message for today of the importance of care by other Christians when we are sick and diseased.

So, the church is always to be concerned about all who are sick and afflicted in our midst. Physical needs are not to be ignored in some misguided understanding of the spiritual nature of the church. On the other hand, the church doesn't replace the medical hospital; so, it must never act as if it is unnecessary. Members of a local church should have the mentality of spiritual doctors and nurses, seeking to care for all with physical sickness. Our hearts should well up with compassion as we see people afflicted. If our Savior was greatly concerned for people with all sorts of diseases, then so should his people be. As will be outlined in the next section of this chapter, there are so many things the church offers to the diseased, disabled, and disordered. To not bring our physical needs to the local church denies the vital work of the church as the hospital of the Great Physician.

In the Hospital Together

In a hospital, most patients tend to suffer alone. Sick individuals are tended to by the medical staff as they wait, rest, and heal in their own beds and rooms. Some of these patients are blessed to have family and friends who will visit them and assist in their care. But on the whole, the individual residing in the hospital is alone, fighting to move from disease to health. How much better is the local church-as-hospital! Since we are connected as the body of Christ, Christians should never suffer alone. The apostle Paul teaches this truth so clearly to us:

> On the contrary, the parts of the body that seem
> to be weaker are indispensable, and on those
> parts of the body that we think less honorable we
> bestow the greater honor, and our unpresentable
> parts are treated with greater modesty, which our
> more presentable parts do not require. But God
> has so composed the body, giving greater honor
> to the part that lacked it, that there may be no
> division in the body, but that the members may
> have the same care for one another.
>
> (1 Corinthians 12:22-25)

The church-as-hospital ensures that there is no division in the body between those who are physically healthy and those who are diseased. Why? So that all receive equal care by one another!

Then, there is the all-important verse 26 which we have already read: "If one member suffers, all suffer together; if one member is honored, all rejoice together" (1 Corinthians 12:26). When there is a true understanding of the church as the undivided body of Christ, we all suffer together when just one of us suffers. Do you believe that? More importantly, do we, as Christians in the local church, live that reality out on a regular basis? The apostle Paul is describing a spiritual truth that is very difficult to consistently enact, because of our sin. Just like patients in a medical hospital, we too often suffer all alone. Christians can easily forget our connectedness, or simply not really want to enter into the suffering of others as we are called to. While suffering is something we usually want to avoid at all costs, being part of the body of Christ is supposed to keep us suffering with one another. We can't just rejoice together when one member is honored; we are to weep with those who weep as well.

Therefore, God uses our physical sicknesses to connect us to one another. Diseases are supposed to not just draw us closer to Christ, but to his body as well. As Tim Chester and Steve Timmis put it, "By becoming a Christian, I belong to God and I belong to my brothers and sisters. It is not that I belong to God and then make a decision to join a local church. My being in Christ means being in Christ with those who are in Christ."[38] Maybe you have witnessed this dynamic occurring when a fringe member of the church becomes ill, enjoys the care of the congregation, and later becomes a much more "core" member of the church. In my church, one of our members was diagnosed with an aggressive cancer which understandably rocked his young family's world. Up until the appearance of that dreaded disease, they were faithful Sunday morning churchgoers, yet disconnected from the other vital church ministries (children's, youth, Sunday school, etc.). As we like say to in the southern states, they were "loved on" to such a degree by so many in the congregation that their view of the church changed. Instead of viewing the church as just a place to attend worship and connect to a few people, this entire family, touched by the disease of cancer, built stronger relationships and became more consistently involved in almost all aspects of body life.

Satan, as the great divider, uses disease in an attempt to separate, isolate, and ultimately destroy people. For those who live in this fallen world without Christ, disease will only bring despair—if it does not end up drawing them to Christ and his church. Enter the church-as-hospital, fighting back in the spiritual war against the world, sin, and Satan. Connected to one another, Christians share in each other's suffering. Connecting the spiritual and the physical, we prioritize spiritual healing while not neglecting to offer care for physical diseases. Recognizing that we are soldiers of Christ in this war, we offer daily comfort and care, binding up one another's wounds. In the end, we know that congregational care in the church-as-hospital keeps us from being divided and alone in our suffering. The body of Christ is called to care for all who are diseased, disabled, and disordered, by the grace of God, and in submission to essential work of the Great Physician.

The Practice of Congregational Care in the Church

Understanding that the church is a hospital requires Christians to engage in vibrant and energetic congregational care for those touched by diseases, disabilities and disorders. What we know in principle must move to gospel-driven practice, as is reflected throughout the New Testament. One of the most convicting stories Jesus told his disciples and which teaches this truth is the parable of the sheep and the goats. Read again the words of King Jesus:

> *Then the King will say to those on his right,*
> *"Come, you who are blessed by my Father,*
> *inherit the kingdom prepared for you from the*
> *foundation of the world. For I was hungry and*
> *you gave me food, I was thirsty and you gave me*
> *drink, I was a stranger and you welcomed me,*

> *I was naked and you clothed me, I was sick and*
> *you visited me, I was in prison and you came*
> *to me."*
>
> (Matthew 25:34-36)

The "sheep" were incredulous, not remembering doing any of these acts of hospitality for the King. Jesus then offers the explanation: "And the King will answer them, 'Truly, I say to you, as you did it to one of the least of these my brothers, you did it to me'" (Matthew 25:40). And there we have the connection: Offering tangible, hospitable and hospital-like care for our brothers and sisters is how we serve King Jesus. So let us, as the church, consider the practical, systematic way to offer congregational care to those who are suffering.

ELDERS AND PRAYER

According to 1 Timothy 3 and Titus 1, the local church has been given the gift of elders to oversee and to shepherd the local congregation. As was referenced earlier, one of the many responsibilities elders have is found in James 5:

> *Is anyone among you sick? Let him call for the*
> *elders of the church, and let them pray over him,*
> *anointing him with oil in the name of the Lord.*
> *And the prayer of faith will save the one who is*
> *sick, and the Lord will raise him up. And if he has*
> *committed sins, he will be forgiven.*
>
> (James 5:14-15)

Elders are called to pray for physical healing as well as for the salvation of souls and forgiveness of sins. Anointing oil is to be used as both a sign of medicinal help and the designation of the work of the Holy Spirit. Prayer for the sick is an essential work of the church, led first by the elders of the church.

So, what specifically are elders praying for when they are praying for people who are suffering with any of the 3-Ds? They are commanded to pray for the Lord to "raise up" the individual, providing healing for the body. This is one aspect which makes praying for the diseased qualitatively different than praying for the disabled or the disordered. When we pray for people with disabilities, we are not usually praying for healing (other than for subsequent illnesses or diseases that come upon them because of the disability); but, instead, we are praying more for their accessibility needs, comfort, and some respite from their suffering. When we pray for people with disorders, we may be praying for physical healing as well as for biblical change and growth in Christ. Whether a disease, disability, or disorder, the elders also pray for such people's salvation and forgiveness of their sins.

Unfortunately, this important instruction concerning the physical and spiritual welfare of sufferers given by James is often ignored in today's congregations. With our modern minds, we think we only need physicians and medicine to take care of our diseases, rendering the local church unnecessary. Church members who are told by James to "call for the elders of the church" may feel that the laying on of hands and prayer is basically ineffective. Other Christians want to keep their diseases private. Many just give lip service to the power of prayer, and only seek it when the disease is extreme or life-threatening. Or, they don't want to bother the elders for something so selfish. On the other hand, elders of the church may not see praying for the sick as their regular duty. Some may just see elders as a board of directors and not a team of spiritual men who care for the flock. Whatever the reason, the neglect by elders of praying for church members who have diseases is simply disobedience to God's Word. The lack of prayer not only denies the power of God to heal our sickness, but it disconnects our physical bodies from our non-physical souls.

PASTORS AND VISITATION

As elders, the ordained pastors of the local church also bear the responsibility of praying for members of their congregation who are diseased. Another related duty of the pastor is to visit the sick, traditionally referred to as "hospital visitation." When we conceive of the local church-as-hospital, then the pastor is essentially bringing hospital care to the hospital! While visiting the sick in the hospital certainly includes prayer, this time should not be limited to a quick drop-in and a brief prayer.

Bringing Christ's hospital to the local medical hospital can be conceived of as *reverse hospitality*. Instead of the sick person being welcomed into the hospitable church, the pastor is entering the sick person's temporary home, bringing warmth, sympathy, and kindness with him. Sitting and talking with the suffering individual and his or her family communicates the relational and hospitable work of the church. The sick in our churches must not languish alone in a hospital, but still feel connected to the rest of the body of Christ.

As I suggested in Chapter 2, my weakest area of ministry as a member of the pastoral staff of my church has always been hospital visitation. There are just too many sick people in hospitals! Seriously, it is a mystery to me why I'm so uncomfortable with people who are diseased when I am much more at home with those who have disorders and disabilities. Maybe it's the extreme weakness and vulnerability a person has when in a hospital bed, which then exposes my fears of being in that state one day. Maybe it's the feeling of inadequacy—that I don't have much to offer like I do for someone who enters my counseling office. Or, could it just be simple selfishness, that it is a sacrifice of my all-important time to go to the hospital and sit, wait, pray, and visit. In my faithless times, it can seem like there isn't much accomplished when we are just hanging out with the sick in the hospital. Do any of these stubborn-heart resistances resonate with you?

If you are a pastor, hopefully you do not share my aversion to visiting people in the hospital but are effectively involved in this important task. Yet it does seem that members of our congregations who are suffering with sicknesses and illnesses are not as cared for as they were in the past. Again, this may be the case because of our reliance of medical professionals to provide for all of our disease care. And, sometimes, there are members of our congregations who don't really desire a pastoral visit, preferring to be private with their own families. Or, maybe the busyness of our culture tempts us to not take the time to visit with and pray for the sick—we'll just send them a get-well-quick text or a social media message. Whatever the reason for the declining regular practice of hospital visitation, the opportunity for ministry, service, and relationship is missed. But when we believe that the church is the hospital, the church must be committed to extend that spiritual hospital to the medical hospital. Our pastors should not forget people who are sick and diseased—the very ones in our congregations who have great need for connectedness in times of possible isolation.

DEACONS AND MERCY MINISTRY

Where elders and pastors are dedicated to the ministry of the Word of God and prayer, deacons are called to come alongside them in order to serve (Acts 6). The very name *deacon* means "servant," revealing the primary responsibility to serve the local church in very practical ways. Of the various duties of the diaconate, many of them fall into the category of the offering of works of mercy—providing help for the poor, needy, orphans, and widows. This vital work of mercy ministry also includes care for individuals who are suffering with all sorts of diseases, disabilities, and disorders. As the word "mercy" infers, deacons serve the more difficult of suffering situations—most often people with chronic diseases or severely debilitating diseases. As elders pray for the sick, deacons come alongside their fellow church members and look for material ways to serve. For while the person with a disease needs prayer first and foremost, he or she also needs care for tangible, basic life needs, including those of his or her family.

In what sorts of ways do our local church deacons serve people who are suffering with the 3-Ds? As they are typically charged with oversight of the finances of the congregation, it makes sense that deacons would focus first on the financial needs of the sick. Are there hospital or medical bills that a member of the congregation is struggling to pay? Or maybe long-term medical bills of the disabled which have made it difficult to pay for day-to-day expenses? The deacons of the church should be poised and ready to offer financial relief when finances are making the suffering that much more worrisome. Certainly, wisdom must be exercised in how much to help and how such financial assistance fits in the context of overall stewardship of God's resources. But to shirk from this tangible act of mercy is yet another way that communicates that the church is not really Christ's hospital, but just a gathering of Christians who are practically independent of one another.

After the financial mercy shown, deacons should creatively look for various other ways to serve the sick. For those with diseases, disabilities, or disorders which have caused them to be bedridden, deacons can enlist teams that will mow lawns, clean houses, and take care of basic home maintenance. Special concern must be shown to sick individuals who are also single, widowed, or without extended family. In a similar way to what is taught us concerning the original deacons in Acts 6, the most vulnerable in our midst need diaconal care. When our deacons act with true hospitality, they are really seeking to serve in any way possible. Those in our churches who are suffering need to know that their deacons are ready to give them tangible help in all things connected to the present trial.

WOMEN'S MINISTRY AND HOSPITALITY

We live in a time where there is much confusion about gender, as well as great trepidation of being labeled as "sexist" when attempting to make any significant kind of distinction between men and women. That fear and confusion often carries over into the evangelical church as well, with our ongoing debates of what women may and may not do in the church. Understandably, the specific focus of these arguments is mainly on what roles and activities women traditionally have *not* been permitted to do in our churches—like being ordained as deacons, elders, or pastors. Wherever your church stands on the debate of what women *can't* do (according to God's Word), it's unfortunate that we typically end up minimizing all the marvelous and essential roles and tasks that women *can* do! Above all other ministries, women in the church are the best at providing hospitality. In much the same way as most wives are more hospitable in and with their homes than their husbands, the women in the church are usually more gifted and skilled in hospitality as well. Yes, I know, someone just labeled me a sexist for making such a generalization!

So, what does a woman's touch in the work of church-as-hospital look like? Women are to be engaged in practical and merciful activities that are in response to the present need. What happens when a mother with small children develops breast cancer? Women in the church can enter into that suffering to provide meals for her family. Childcare may be required while mom is receiving treatment, because dad has to keep working to stay gainfully employed. And what about care for the home when mom is at her weakest? Teams of women can clean the house and do laundry—bringing peace and comfort to the home. Again, this is a case of reverse hospitality—where the church-as-hospital enters the home to be hosts and give rest. When individuals in the local church are connected to one another, we share our presence in our homes—refusing to be isolationists—and not letting our pride keep our brothers and sisters from caring for us.

Women's ministry in the church is tasked to work side by side with the church deacons, as fellow servants of Christ. When a young father is diagnosed with a brain tumor, the deacons should jump in to examine the financial needs, both current and future. The young wife who is also impacted by her husband's disease—who has been homeschooling her children—now has to go back to work. Therefore, the deacons may step in and help pay for some of the children's schooling for the first year. They also might gather volunteers to take care of the yard. Working in harmony with the deacons, women's ministry mobilizes to offer childcare after school, until the mother gets off work. A month's worth of freezer meals may be just what the doctor ordered to get the family adjusted to the new realities this disease has produced. Again, the ways women can serve those who are suffering is as individualized and personal as the care received in a medical hospital.

Let's also make sure to not disconnect service from body of Christ relationships when it comes to hospitality and mercy ministry for the sick. Remember, the church is uniquely designed to deal with physical needs as well as spiritual needs! As the women of the church are offering hospitality to families touched by disease, they also have the opportunity to get to know one another. How easy it is to serve someone without really entering into that person's suffering! Women can be more focused on being "Marthas" (Luke 10:38-42) who are busy doing works of service and forget to sit and visit and engage with families touched by disease, disability, or disorder—showing them Jesus. Remember, Christians are to mourn with those who mourn, which implies that we actually are connected in care and compassion. Individuals involved in women's ministry do works of mercy; this then becomes a vehicle of loving people with the love of Christ.

MOBILIZING THE CONGREGATION

If you look back at the title of this chapter, you'll notice that it isn't "elder care," "pastoral care," or "diaconal care" which is the work of the church-as-hospital. Certainly, pastors, elders, deacons, and other church staff members are to take the lead in providing aid and care for people who are suffering. But if we only look to our leaders to do all the care, will we truly be offering hospitality to all who need it? The correct model of congregationally based ministry is summarized in Ephesians 4: "And he gave the apostles, the prophets, the evangelists, the shepherds and teachers, to equip the saints for the work of ministry, for building up the body of Christ . . ." (Ephesians 4:11-12). The entire congregation is to be mobilized and equipped to do the work of ministry, in order to give health to the entire body of Christ. All church members are to be the eyes and ears, and the hands and feet of Christ in the work of caring for sufferers. When the church adopts the world's view of only the few "professionals" doing all the work, the job won't get done, and the body will stay disconnected, weak, and frail.

Therefore, the elders are called to mobilize the congregation to pray for the sick. While the elders lay hands and anoint the diseased with oil, church members join in prayer on a daily basis—corporately and individually. While the pastors visit the sick, they also encourage members to do their Matthew 25 duty of caring for the least of Christ's sheep. The deacons take the lead in serving the practical needs of individuals with diseases, enlisting the help of those with financial resources and special skills who can help those with all the needs. The hospitality of the women of the church serves as an example to the entire congregation on a week-to-week basis. Rounding out our hospital analogy, it's not just the doctors and nurses and med-techs who are tasked with the work of healing—it's also the other patients who must care for one another. The presence of disease, disability, and disorder in our lives in this fallen world is to be the great motivator for us to love and serve each other in ways that we typically don't when all is well.

A final passage that we should drink in deeply, with our minds on all who suffer in our midst, is found in Romans 12:

Love one another with brotherly affection. Outdo
one another in showing honor. Do not be slothful
in zeal, be fervent in spirit, serve the Lord. Rejoice
in hope, be patient in tribulation, be constant
in prayer. Contribute to the needs of the saints
and seek to show hospitality. Bless those who
persecute you; bless and do not curse them.
Rejoice with those who rejoice, weep with those
who weep. Live in harmony with one another.
Do not be haughty, but associate with the lowly.
Never be wise in your own sight.

(Romans 12:10-16)

How's that for a list of responsibilities for the local church! More importantly, what kind of church would we have if we regularly obeyed these commands? And, right in the center of these essential instructions is verse 13: "Contribute to the needs of the saints and seek to show hospitality." When it comes to caring for people with diseases, disabilities, and disorder, we have the beautiful opportunity to love with brotherly affection, and outdo one another in showing honor. As Yong proclaims: "Ministry to people with profound disabilities becomes a means of ministering the love of God with them in an otherwise inhospitable world."[39]

For Personal Reflection

1. Think about the last time you were hospitalized. What were things that made the stay a positive one, and what were things that made it more negative? Did your experience change the way you look at people who are suffering chronically with disease?

2. When you are sick, what do you want most from the people closest to you? What about when you are spiritually sick?

3. Assess your desire to visit people who are diseased— whether in a hospital, in a nursing home, in hospice, or even at home. Other than those visits you are "required" to make, what keeps you from visiting people you know more often?

4. Consider why people appreciate being visited while suffering with a disease. While many appear to want to be alone, think about the spiritual value of visitation.

5. How would you grade your hospitality personally and as a family? Who is regularly in your home, other than family and close friends? If you asked members in your church, would they consider you to be a hospitable person?

For Church Assessment

1. Evaluate the overall work of your church in the vital ministry area of congregational care. In some churches, care for the sick gets left to the pastors or elders. Does your church have a vision for every member caring for those with diseases?

2. Do your elders spend time in corporate prayer for the sick? In what ways can they grow in this vital task?

3. Is your pastoral staff involved in the visitation of all who are sick? Is this a high value ministry for your pastors? Do the people who are suffering believe that they are being cared for by their pastors, or that it is a burden for them?

4. Evaluate how responsive the deacons of your church are to the needs of all who are suffering. Is money well spent in caring for people who are struggling to pay their medical bills? Think about ways the deacons, using their time and gifts, might care for the sick.

5. Assess how much time and energy the women of the church give to caring for those who are suffering. What systems need to improve so that more hospitality and comfort are given to those stricken with disease?

6. How is your congregation caring for one another? Think about the ways that every church member can be equipped to minister to the sick and suffering.

For Group Discussion

1. How does the church-as-hospital not eliminate the need for actual medical care?

2. How does the etymology of the word "hospital" help us to understand the church as a hospital?

3. According to Hebrews 13:2, what should motivate us to be hospitable?

4. How is the church both a hospital for our spiritual health as well as our physical health?

5. How and why are the elders to pray for people who are suffering?

6. Why are hospital visitations such an important work of the local church?

7. How are deacons charged to serve those who are suffering?

8. How are the women in the church uniquely called to help?

9. Why must the entire local church congregation be involved in the work of church-as-hospital?

CHAPTER 5

THE CHURCH AS A FAMILY

Disability Ministry in the Church

A s exciting as it was to go on my first foreign mission trip at the age of eighteen, I still remember the sense of relief I experienced when our team was able to eat dinner at a Pizza Hut. It wasn't primarily the pizza that gave me comfort, but much more the fact that it was all *so familiar*. The building looked the same as the one in my hometown. The menu was pretty much identical as well. The only difference was that we Americans were eating with our hands instead of forks! Don't we all seek what is familiar, especially when life is most difficult? Just think about the word "familiar" for a moment. It has the same Latin root as *family*, with the original definition being "intimate, very friendly, on a family footing." Then, the secondary definition emerged later, of which we are more "familiar": "known from long association."[40] With these definitions in mind, our desire for the familiar is really the longing for family! And one of the best pictures of the church we have in the New Testament is the church as a familiar family.

The Picture of a Familial Church
ORPHANS, ISOLATION, INDEPENDENCE

We live in a time where it seems like many of our technological advancements end up serving to separate people rather than connect them. Added to that, the focus of much of the marketing of these gadgets is on how they allow us to choose our own (personalized and individualized) music, movies, shows, and gaming. This scheme works because, of our own choosing, we tend to seek independence and isolation rather than interdependence and relationship. Even though God puts us into families from birth, then into various friendships and communities—and potentially even into marriages—our sinful hearts can fight regularly against intimacy. God declared it is not good for man to be alone (Genesis 2:18), yet privacy, separateness, and independence often seems preferable and comfortable. Adam and Eve's first impulse after their original sin was to hide from God and to even seek independence from each other! We modern humans, enabled by our technology and sifted through our sinful, fearful hearts, continue to find ways to enter into relationships without really being *in* relationships. Unfortunately, Christians who are given all sorts of opportunities for family and community by God can be just as bad at choosing isolation as non-Christians.

Of course, we are speaking in broad generalizations here. There are also many people all around us who crave relationships every day, and, for one reason or another, are excluded. Widows and divorcees may wish to be married again. Orphans dream of having parents who love them. Older people can become very lonely, as friends and family are no longer with them. And then, on top of all that, we have people suffering with diseases, disabilities, and disorders. Whether it is difficulty communicating, uniqueness in thinking and feeling, or barriers in mobility, suffering individuals can most easily become isolated and disconnected from other people.

For the many who long for relationships, people aren't available to help them overcome their obstacles to true community. Then there are those with particular disabilities or diseases who are too often perceived as being unable to relate to others because of their impairments; so they sadly end up having little human contact in their lives. According to the American Psychological Association, loneliness and social isolation can be a greater threat to our health than obesity.[41]

Into this tragic mixture of orphan-impulse, isolation, and independence (that we either seek or don't seek), God sent his Son, Jesus Christ, to be *God with us*. What a glorious truth that enables Christians to never be alone and isolated again! As a byproduct of this intimacy with his people, he then calls his people to be in a familial relationship with one another as the church of Jesus Christ. While we were once orphans in this world, Christians are adopted in Christ and become children of God:

> *See what kind of love the Father has given to us,*
> *that we should be called children of God; and so we*
> *are. The reason why the world does not know us*
> *is that it did not know him. Beloved, we are God's*
> *children now, and what we will be has not yet*
> *appeared; but we know that when he appears we*
> *shall be like him, because we shall see him as he is.*
>
> *(1 John 3:1-2)*

It is the amazing love of God that not only makes us his children, but gathers his children together into the church-as-family. As the apostle Paul writes: "For through him we both have access in one Spirit to the Father. So then you are no longer strangers and aliens, but you are fellow citizens with the saints and members of the household of God . . ." (Ephesians 2:18-19). By its very existence, the church of Jesus Christs fights against our isolation and independence, whether we like it or not. Since the Christian is not an orphan, he or she so should never act like one *or* be treated by other believers as one.

Where Everybody Knows My Name

One of my favorite mindless '80s TV sitcoms I enjoyed as a teenager was *Cheers*, where the characters spent most of their time in a Boston bar. Its theme song still echoes in my mind, especially when we consider the church-as-family. Here is the opening stanza (sing along if you know it):

> *Making your way in the world today takes everything you've got.*
> *Taking a break from all your worries, sure would help a lot.*
> *Wouldn't you like to get away?*
> *Sometimes you want to go*
> *Where everybody knows your name,*
> *and they're always glad you came.*
> *You wanna be where you can see,*
> *our troubles are all the same*
> *You wanna be where everybody knows your name.*[42]

The folks at the *Cheers* bar fully embraced this sentiment, as they acted like a family, shared their troubles with one another, and lived life together—even in their unique personalities. Now, while I will be careful not to hold out a neighborhood pub as the example for our local churches, it's important to see how many other places and institutions also strive to be a family. And, unfortunately, sometimes they can actually do a better job at family life than the many of our Christian congregations.

If the *Cheers* theme song is simply expressing a widely held sentiment, why are we attracted to places and groups "where everybody knows your name?" First, it certainly expresses relationship, as well as a level of intimacy. Think about how uncomfortable it is when you see someone at church that you *should* know by name, but you have forgotten it. An awkward, "Hey . . . brother . . ." is the best you can do! But do you ever forget the names of those family members closest to you (except for a temporary brain cramp)? Knowing one another's name communicates that we have a relationship with one another.

To have our name spoken by another means that I am known by him or her. It's the starting point to the intimacy that naturally comes in family life. So, what does it say about Christians when we don't even try to learn each other's name? As harsh as it sounds, it says: "I don't really want to know you."

Having a place where everyone knows your name also has to do with identity. Just think about your last name. It denotes family and belonging, doesn't it? We are Kwasnys, and we live together in the Kwasny home. All God's adopted children are Christians, and they are chosen to "live" together in the church. With identity is supposed to come belonging. Yet, in many places, the church of Jesus Christ looks more like a fraternal organization, where isolated individuals and biological families simply gather to worship God. In other words, we all share certain beliefs, certain activities, and a particular building for a short period of time—then find our main identity and belonging in other places with other people. So is that God's plan for all who take the name "Christian?" Are we just adopted into the heavenly family of God, yet to remain separate during our days on earth? In our modern times where even the natural family is becoming more and more disconnected, maybe the church-as-family is increasingly unrealistic.

Yet, just because our sinfulness and weakness can make us quite ineffective at familial relationships at times does not negate the fact that Christians are connected with the same name. We *are* brothers and sisters in Christ if Jesus Christ is truly our elder brother. As God himself says: "Fear not, for I have redeemed you; I have called you by name, you are mine" (Isaiah 43:1). Christians don't get to choose the people who are going to be adopted into their family. God alone decides, calls, and adopts who will become part of his family. And we know from Scripture that his children come from every nation, tribe, and tongue, as well as every socioeconomic strata and culture. Extrapolating further, we also understand that there are people with all sorts of diseases, disabilities, and disorders in the family of God. Therefore, we must strive to become a place where everybody knows each other's name!

WE NEED EACH OTHER . . . REALLY

Writing on why modern people still need each other, two psychologists at USC made this assessment:

Humans, because of necessity, evolved into social beings. Dependence on and cooperation with each other enhanced our ability to survive under harsh environmental circumstances. Although the survival threats of these circumstances have lessened in today's world, people continue to have a need to affiliate with others. Indeed, the lack of such connections can lead to many problems. . . .[43]

While this is a valiant attempt to understand why people actually need each other, it is a textbook case of false, evolutionary thinking. Humans didn't evolve into social beings; they were created by a relational God in relationships, and for relationships. Dependence on and cooperation with each other certainly enhanced our ability to survive, but it did much more than that. Most importantly, it reflected the relationship of the three persons of the Trinity, allowing us to love and care for one another, and grow in Christ. Finally, it is also mistaken to think that our "survival threats" have lessened in modern times. Where people may imagine that they are more able to exist alone, the threats to our survival have always been the same. Christians need other Christians so that we can live safely as God's family!

One of the main indicators that a family is not spiritually or emotionally healthy is when individual members don't recognize that they actually need each other. Think of what was communicated by the prodigal son to his father in the Luke 15 parable: *"Dad, I don't need you, my brother, or the rest of my family; I just want your money and my freedom."* The prodigal clearly didn't recognize his need to be a functioning member of his family. He may have thought that family life was just slowing him down—an obstacle to his peace and joy. Of course, according to Jesus, that prodigal son represents you and me when we reject God as our Father—preferring to give ourselves over to the supposed freedom the world has to offer. The truth is, when we come to believe that we don't need God, we also end up thinking we don't need the family of God! Or, it can work the other way too—when we don't think we need the family of God, we are acting like we don't need God either.

Just think for a moment how members of the family of God can act like we really don't need each other in the local church. On the practical level of church family life, church members can be sporadic in their attendance, especially during certain sports seasons or when they and their children have more important activities. Then, there are members of the local church who don't want anyone to know that they are sick, in the hospital, or suffering a health issue. Still others don't want the pastor or other church members to know of their marriage or parenting struggles. And, what about the time required for friendships in the church? Those relationships can often be satisfied outside of the church family. Then, tack on to all of these phenomena the challenge that people seem to be so much busier than ever before in human history, and that translates to church life not being really needed. In the end, many Christians come to believe they can grow in Christ just fine without real, Christian, family fellowship.

What do Christians actually need from their church family? We certainly need the preaching and teaching of the Word of God, right? But, in this modern age, we can get all of that at home—on television, radio, or streaming through the Internet. We need opportunities to serve God and be a witness to the world for Jesus. But we can also do that on our own, outside of the local church, or through parachurch organizations. We need regular times and places to worship God. But can't we worship all by ourselves, in our homes, or with our biological families? We may also have the need for counseling, aid, and support from other people. Not to beat a dead horse, but can't we find help in all sorts of places other than the church? We should recognize our need for finding all of this within our local church family, but we can convince ourselves that the church won't meet these needs, or other organizations and groups can do it better.

So, what was left off this short list of "needs" that the church can provide? Christian fellowship, for one! Sure, we can find friendships outside of a local church, and we often do. But a localized family of God offers a built-in, ready-made laboratory of relationships in which we are called to enter and participate.

We need to be in fellowship with other Christians. We need to be in fellowship with Christians who are not all like us. We need Christian fellowship that is not exactly of our own choosing. We need the variety, diversity, and heterogeneity of the local church. Yes, this is a *spiritual need*, not an option. Our walk with Christ needs it. Our sanctification requires it. Our natural sin habit to stay within our comfort zone demands it. The local church gives us the Christian fellowship that we need. And that is true even though the church is made up of difficult people (ourselves included). Christians must connect with this real need in order to transform the church into a biblically functional family.

All who are "in Christ" need Christian fellowship. How much more is this true for individuals with "special" needs? Certainly, we typically refer to individuals with disabilities as having special needs because of the assistance required for full inclusion and accessibility. While those are true and special needs, it can also be argued that their greater spiritual need is the *need for Christian fellowship!* This is a special need because, even though all Christians have this need, people with disabilities have restrictions or impairments that make relationships just that much harder. Disabilities, like disorders and diseases, can isolate rather than connect us to others. So while we often recognize the practical needs of those with special needs, we must not miss the need for true Christian family.

Sharing Our Lives as Family

One of the earliest lessons taught to children by their parents (after "Obey your parents," of course) is: *Share your toys.* There's no greater picture of self-centeredness than a youngster clutching his or her favorite plaything with white knuckles, screaming: "Mine, mine!" The wise parent will attempt to put a stop to this behavior by training the child to give and share, instead of just take and exclude. So, why is this such an important lesson to teach—and to learn? For one thing, it's because sharing isn't natural. We come out of the womb loving ourselves first, not other people. We have to learn that this is not the way to live in relationships in this world.

And, it's vital to learn, because an adult who doesn't share moves from being immature and foolish to being self-absorbed and isolated. One important way Christians connect to each other as the family of God is by sharing all good things with one another.

Once again, we see this important aspect of the church-as-family taught in the pages of Scripture. The early church, forged in the fires of persecution and suffering, understood the need to share with one another: "And all who believed were together and had all things in common. And they were selling their possessions and belongings and distributing the proceeds to all, as any had need" (Acts 2:44-45). What a beautiful picture of a congregational life of sharing! Believers in Jesus were "together" and had "all things in common." Is that hard to imagine? Now, this example is not given to us to instruct us into some sort of forced communism. These early believers shared in very practical ways, having all things in common, by their own volition—out of love for Christ and one another. The sharing which demonstrates our connectedness as the family of God isn't just about selling our possessions and making sure everyone has the same amount of stuff. What it really means is that Christians are to have hearts that share our *entire lives*— our joys and sorrows, our abundance and our poverty, our problems and our successes, our sickness and health. Sharing is to characterize church life.

So, why is sharing in the church required, and not just optional? Because it reminds us that none of us has everything that we need—spiritually speaking. At places in our Christian walk, we can buy into the idea that "all I need is Jesus." While it is true that Jesus is all we need for salvation, we need the family of God in our sanctification. As Timothy Lane and Paul Tripp succinctly put it: "As isolated individuals, we cannot reach the level of maturity God has designed for us. . . . Our personal transformation must be worked out within the family of God."[44] We share our lives because we are not orphans. We share our lives to move from independence to interdependence. We share our lives because it is necessary. As we learn to share with one another, the more mature and unified in Christ we become.

All in the Family

A healthy, functional family strives to include *all* members of the family in every aspect of family life. Families, when they are operating as they should, love one another—not loving some members, hating others, and disregarding still others. A sound family works toward unity, not division—and experiences great grief and despair when one member is separate, lost, and disconnected. Now, I know what you're thinking—division, disconnectedness, and a lack of love occur in biological families all the time! Yes, due to the reality of sin and human weakness, family members are regularly unloved, unaccepted, left out, and ignored. Siblings fight each other, children hate their parents, and parents fail their children. So, maybe most of our churches are acting like a typical family after all—a flawed, sinful, disconnected family. But hopefully, as believers, we understand that we must heed the call to include all those who join our church as family members.

Of all the 3-Ds, a person suffering with a recognizable disease will often find it relatively easy to be accepted as part of the church family. Can we say the same for people with mental and emotional disorders? According to Smietana, "Churches talk openly about cancer, diabetes, heart attacks and other health conditions—they should do the same for mental illness, in order to reduce the sense of stigma."[45] More and more research appears to be demonstrating that people with disorders are suffering in silence in the pews, feeling misunderstood and left out.[46] While many mental and emotional disorders are hidden from plain sight, what happens when they are talked about and brought to light? Are fellow believers, even with their disorders, accepted and embraced as full-fledged family members or more like the "crazy aunt" nobody in your family talks about?

What about people with disabilities? When I was first hired in my present church staff position, an elder and his wife challenged me with these haunting words: "Are you interested in ministering to *all* the children in this church, or just *most* of them?" This hurting couple had been at the church for almost thirty years, watching their daughter with special needs being routinely left out, excluded, and isolated.

There were now five young families touched by disability in our church. Would they also be pushed to the edges of the church family? More importantly, as a ministry leader, would I ensure that these families are embraced as true family members? The point is that, when a church conscientiously desires to grow as a family, the eyes of individual Christians are opened to the needs of *all* family members. When we are convicted that *all* are essential, we will see people with diseases, disabilities, or disorders who are being ignored. We will notice people who desire to be part of the family, but have obstacles that must be reduced or eliminated. We make the church both familial and familiar!

The Practice of Disability Ministry in the Church

There are many ministries in the local church that are focused on enfolding people into the family of God. Youth ministry, children's ministry, and men's and women ministries all work to connect people to one another, building relationships as the body of Christ. Discipleship ministries, mercy ministries, music ministries, and outreach ministries are also forums for church members to grow and serve together as brothers and sisters in Christ. Yet, all of these examples of ministries in the church tend to assume that people are fully capable to enter into familial relationships, if desired. But what if a person is excluded? What if someone lacks access? What if special assistance is required? *This is why every local church needs a disability ministry.* It is the vital work of the church to ensure that *all* members are welcomed into the family. Without a disability ministry, our churches will be something less than a fully functional family. So while people with diseases and disorders also need to be embraced as family, those who suffer with disability have a unique need. Typically excluded, restricted, and limited, these individuals and families require a special focus to draw them into family life. So, the practice of disability ministry is the "poster child" for the church-as-family.

Practicing Full Inclusion

Researching emotional pain in social settings, David Oberleitner observed: "[Being excluded] is a pretty universal experience: when you raise your hand in class and aren't called on; if you're ignored in a professional setting; when children are left out of games on the playground . . . "[47] So, if exclusion is something we all experience at one point or another in our lives, we should all understand the pain that is involved—as well as the joy that comes with inclusion. Oftentimes, the fear and shame of exclusion is what motivates us to do whatever it takes to find a way "in." But what about an impulse to help others to be included? As Christians, we are called to more than just help—and rather, to ensure that the people who are excluded are included. This is the first and main practice of disability ministry. The ministry exists to have its eyes on the entire church family, and make sure no one is excluded.

Inclusion must be more than a heartfelt desire or an educational philosophy—it must be an active, consistent practice. In his study of the church and disability, McNair asserts: ". . . there are many churches where overt exclusion is occurring, and exponentially more where the exclusion by default is happening. . . ."[48] As we considered in a previous chapter, inclusion for all people with disabilities begins by becoming a welcoming, inviting church. After all, what sort of family refuses to receive people into their home? As Christians, we take our lead from the Lord Jesus: "When the crowds learned it, they followed him, and he welcomed them and spoke to them of the kingdom of God and cured those who had need of healing" (Luke 9:11). The body of Christ must welcome other believers into their local families because Christ welcomed us into *his* family in the first place! Being a welcoming body is not an option, but a joy that comes from experiencing the welcoming love of Christ.

And what is the essential activity of church life that people must feel most welcomed into by the family of God? The corporate worship service on the Lord's Day morning stands as the seminal activity of the church family. All must be welcomed and encouraged to participate in the worship service. Unfortunately, there is typically not full agreement among church leaders that individuals with disabilities can or should be included in worship. After all, we've created children's church primarily because kids are a distraction, or they need to learn to worship on "their own level." That same rationale is often used for individuals with disabilities, thereby excluding them from worship because they are too loud, or they can't understand the sermon. This thinking goes against the principle of the church-as-family. While there are other times and activities that are appropriate for separating people into learning groups, the worship service should remain corporate at all costs. "Welcome to worship," must be declared from the pulpits of our churches, and actually be addressed to *all* who desire to worship God.

To be clear, there will be times where young children and individuals with disabilities need to be temporarily removed from worship because the level of disruption has become too high. Other settings may also be required in order to transition individuals with special needs back to the worship service at a later time. But, as will be addressed in the next sections, finding ways to allow parents to engage in corporate worship while others are caring for their children *in* the worship service is essential. This is a challenge that must be taken up by the family of God. Sadly, there are too many stories of families who are asked to leave the worship service, and even the church, because their child with a disability is thought of as being too difficult. There is no denying that disabilities can present challenges that seem too hard to overcome in church life. But when the biblical truth of the church-as-family is our guiding principle, the practical efforts to make the worship service inclusive is mandatory—even when extremely challenging.

There is a time and place for ministry programs that are tailored for specific special needs. For example, church leaders must make wise decisions about opening up a unique Sunday school class for children or adults with disabilities. Or, possibly a separate midweek Bible study for adults with special needs at their educational level needs to be formed, while the other adults are having small groups of their own. From a purely educational vantage point, it makes sense to provide studies and classes that more closely match particular learning abilities and goals. Having parallel and complementary programs and activities is also a form of inclusion, under the principle of "separate, but equal." These sorts of groups facilitate Christian fellowship with other children, youth, or adults with similar disabilities. Using our natural family model as an example, we can be connected as family members even if we are, at times, relating with our own peer group.

Yet, great care must be given to the practice of real inclusion as well. There should be times in church life when heterogeneous Christian fellowship is prioritized over our learning goals and methodologies. An individual with an intellectual disability may actually need to be in a Sunday school class with his own peer group, instead of at his educational level, in order to enjoy relationships. Or, a teenager who is functioning at a third-grade level will still desperately need to be with other youth his own age at some point. Then there are the other typical ministry programs like choir, small discipleship groups, men and women's Bible studies and activities, prayer groups, etc. The church staff and ministry leaders must be diligent to keep asking themselves how to open these groups to include anyone with a disability. Again, this may involve removing practical, physical barriers, or dealing with the possible distractions and difficulties from people who are more active, make noises, etc. As McNair states: "If it is too much trouble to include persons with severe disability in our churches, what does that shout out to those around us about the God we serve?"[49]

Every Ministry Accessible

One of my first churches as an adult church member was located on some beautiful property with several gorgeous, historic buildings—especially the sanctuary. Unfortunately, most of the church edifices were lacking some very important things: signs. Sure, there was some outdated signage in view, especially gold nameplates with the names of donors who designated their offerings for a particular room or church pew. But most significantly missing were directional signs which pointed the way to some very important locations, such as restrooms. So, because I am one of those men who usually refuse to ask directions, I went almost a year worshiping in a church with no idea of where the restrooms were, or any knowledge if restrooms actually existed. I can still remember the day I "just happened" to stumble across the men's room—exactly at the time I really needed one. The moral of the story is: *All people need accessibility in the church, not just the disabled.* Those with special needs just need much more of it. Thankfully, when a local church embraces the church-as-family, it will properly understand the need for accessibility.

While the practice of welcoming people is certainly rooted in the love of Christ, it is also driven by a desire to make the family of God accessible. If our church buildings happen to be in a dangerous part of town so they have security fencing surrounding them, is that a welcoming message? What about a church parking lot with no handicap spaces, a sanctuary with no reserved wheelchair spots, or no listening devices available for the sermon? These are all essential accessibility practices that, when they are properly in place and operational, say: "You're welcome," to all who come near. Restroom signs help, too! So, a local church must give careful thought to all the ways "strangers" feel unwelcomed, and that includes, at the top of the list, individuals with disabilities. The church should be way out in front of the culture in the zealous effort of making our facilities accessible solely because of our family mindset!

But disability ministry goes far beyond the required accessibility protocols for our buildings mandated by federal and state laws. Churches may have wheelchair spots in the sanctuary, yet have Christians who are unwilling to assist a person in that space sing from the hymnal, or turn the pages of the Scriptures. We may desire to have children with special needs in our church, but end up giving their parents disapproving glares when those children make strange noises or move around too much. Church members may enjoy the young, "cute" children with disabilities, but display overt fear of those in the youth group who are harder to handle. But when we consider all believers as part of the family of God, we are willing to make the church truly accessible for individuals and families with special needs. Welcoming people who are suffering moves us beyond our comfort zones to new heights of Christlike sacrifice we rarely have the opportunity for—but need greatly.

If the local church was just a school, then we would merely make choices of accessibility based on educational plans, needs, and goals. But, just in case we haven't made the point enough: the church is also a family! The right practice of disability ministry seeks to balance times that put education in the forefront and other times that put fellowship front and center. It's vital to get the input of adults with disabilities and parents of children with disabilities to learn how to accomplish accessibility. So, a child may be included in an age-related Sunday school class, but be placed in a midweek Bible study with other children with disabilities. The hard work of evaluating each activity and program, as well as the specific needs of all people with disabilities, will communicate the family message of accessibility *and* inclusion.

THE BUDDY SYSTEM

How do we make the worship services and all the rest of the ministries of the local church both accessible and inclusive? While particular disabilities require regular personal assistants and aides at home and school, the church needs to provide similar help to individuals and families. One way to accomplish this is by the selection and training of "buddies" who will come alongside children, youth, and adults to allow quality inclusion. Do you see how this also fits within the understanding of the church-as-family? Since we are brothers and sisters in Christ, we can assist those with special needs to be able to participate, serve, and learn with and alongside us. And since we are the family of God, we are also friends—buddies who don't just assist, but relate and befriend! Those involved in disability ministry as buddies recognize that accessibility and inclusion most often involve the giving of personal time and relationship.

And, yes, as the heading communicates, buddies need to be organized in a system. Buddies must first be properly chosen—youth and adults who truly desire to love others with the love of Christ. They need to be servants who understand the role of the church as a family, and who will do what it takes to make the kingdom of God accessible. Then, buddies must be trained in an understanding of the individual as well as the effects of his or her specific disability. Much of this is "on-the-job training," as the buddy learns the person's needs, gifts, and skills as they work together. Leaders of the system must then balance when a healthy rotation of buddies is required, and when one specific buddy is the best practice. As a local body is welcoming more and more family members with disabilities into the church, a sophisticated rotation system must be developed. As much as every need possible of the disabled is to be met, the needs of the buddies to stay connected to the rest of church life cannot be neglected either.

A robust buddy system will include children, youth, and adults. While a third grader with severe autism may require an adult buddy in order to initially be in Sunday school, what a joy it becomes when another third grader becomes his regular buddy at a later time. Or, a child with a communication board can have another child his own age help translate the Bible lesson to him in class. Accordingly, teenagers can be enlisted to hang out with other teenage girls and boys with Down syndrome—even on youth trips and retreats. What a beautiful picture of familial love when one adult with a tablet is holding it for another adult with special needs—so she can follow along in worship. Can you envision church family life in operation? Whereas the operating principle in most places in society is "every man for himself," the buddy system exudes the *band of brothers* principle of "no man left behind."

Respite Care

The word "respite" is really such a marvelous word. Its original French and Latin etymology literally means "respect" or "consideration." From that primary meaning, respite has come to mean, "a short time of rest or relief from something difficult or unpleasant."[50] Now, while most of us find plenty of opportunities for respite on a regular basis, a parent of a child with a disability does not. A babysitter can't readily be hired, siblings may not be old enough to step in, and their child may never be able to stay home alone when older. Depending on the disability, it may be nearly impossible for couples to even have a fairly regular date night out together. So, into that need, enter the local church with a profound opportunity to offer some level of regular respite care. And, yes, this is exactly what a well-functioning family would do for one another.

One of the most family-related examples of respite care that can be provided by a local church is a "parents' night out." Even if just for a few hours, parents and other caregivers can leave their children with disabilities and their siblings in the care of the family of God. Do I even have to mention the power and joy of even a little bit of rest from the challenge of caring for loved ones with disabilities? While some parents will plan their own definition of a fun date night, others may simply enjoy walking around a grocery store in peace. Or, a nap may be the most pleasing respite of all! Recognizing the great individual need for regular soul and body enlivening respite should move Christians to build these required times into the DNA of church life. Respite is an incredible way to offer Sabbath rest to parents who feel like they are enslaved to a never-ending task—even though they deeply love their children. Brothers and sisters in Christ can offer a cup of cold water of respite that will feel like an ocean of relief.

As much as respite care is all about giving rest to parents and caregivers, this is not to be understood as mere babysitting for their children, youth, and adults. Individuals with disabilities and their siblings also need respite from their day-to-day grind and work! So a parents' night out respite care event is organized to give the attendees a soul-refreshing balance of play, activity, worship, and fellowship. Much of it should be free time in order to communicate the need for individualized rest. And, yes, many individual buddies will be needed for this church-as-family event. Entire families should be enlisted from the congregation as well, so adults can visit with and assist adults, youth with youth, and children with children. Sometimes, the temptation is to staff these events only with medical or therapeutic professionals. But as the family of God, we all must be involved in providing these times of respite and fellowship in order to build up the body of Christ, serving one another in Christ! Then, all sorts of other respite opportunities can be planned, including very personal care as needed.

ACCESSING GIFTEDNESS

A final basic component of the practice of disability ministry can also be pictured to us by a well-functioning natural family. As our children grow up, most parents enjoy seeing the uniqueness of each one of them. Hopefully, Christian moms and dads don't just focus on their child's sinful proclivities, weaknesses, or inabilities! When parents are paying attention, they can see talents, skills, and gifts within their child's little, unique personalities, that are then to be encouraged and focused in the right direction. And, as children are graciously converted to Christ they will become gifted by the Holy Spirit to be used mightily in the kingdom of God. When God has also given parents a few children or more, they will often get to see how these gifts make them into a well-rounded and balanced family unit.

So, consider what that family dynamic teaches us about our church family. Most Christians are familiar with the New Testament teaching that we all have been given spiritual gifts when we come to Christ. We are given sample lists of these gifts in texts like Romans 12, 1 Corinthians 12, and 1 Peter 4. Unfortunately, in church life, we can act like only a few chosen Christians have spiritual gifts—a sort of "celebrity class" of believers who preach, teach, or serve sacrificially. We've been told for years by the church experts that about 20 percent of church members do 80 percent of the work. Why does this tend to be a truism? It certainly has to do somewhat with priorities; yet, it also illuminates the fact that many Christians believe they lack giftedness. And so we have a dysfunctional church family, where some Christians exercise their gifts regularly, while most are in a congregational underclass, only passively enjoying the gifts of others. Again, this does not reflect the New Testament image of church-as-family.

Therefore, disability ministry must seek out the giftedness of all church members touched by disability. Why is this pursuit often overlooked in our ministries? As Stephanie Hubach states: "All too often, when we focus on people with special needs, we emphasize their specific disability and fail to see their abilities. Of course, all people with disabilities have tangible abilities too. But Christians with disabilities are also fully endowed with spiritual gifts."[51] Do we really believe this scriptural truth? Or, again, do we think spiritual giftedness is only for some sort of highly skilled Christian? In order for disability ministry to be firmly connected to the church-as-family, it must seek to encourage and enable people with disabilities to use all of their gifts in the church. The beauty is that there are so many places to serve. It is truly unfortunate when the local church does not receive and enjoy the blessing of the spiritual gifts of all its members, including those who appear least able and gifted!

Disability ministry is not just some sort of optional program for local churches that just happen to have a certain quota of persons with disabilities already in their midst. Properly seen as providing accessibility and inclusion in the family of God, it's just what the church is all about, in an organic way. The bottom line is that disability ministry is the often-wearying work of doing good to everyone, especially those in the household of faith (Galatians 6:9-10). Through regular events like respite care, we welcome individuals and families to become part of our church family for, at least, a short period of time. Then, as people with disabilities join the church, we have even more opportunity to do good, including them in all aspects of family life. The household of faith should be the preeminent place of accessibility and aid as we seek to include all of our brothers and sisters in Christ!

For Personal Reflection

1. Consider ways you act more like an orphan than a member of the family of God. How does it impact your relationship with God as well as other brothers and sisters in Christ?

2. How important is it that people know your name? While some of us crave to be popular or even famous, being known by those who are important to us has a particular impact in our lives. What exactly is it? And why do we want a good name?

3. Be honest with yourself about your need for other people. Is any Christian truly satisfied with being a "loner"? Think about what keeps you isolated from other Christians around you, or willing to settle for more "surface" relationships.

4. What makes sharing with other Christians such a challenge? Think about why it is easy to work alone than as a team, even when there are great benefits to sharing the work! What makes it even more difficult to share our suffering with others?

5. Think about how disabilities have a way of keeping us on the outside, on the fringe. Do you expect people touched by disabilities to find their own way into the family of God? What are some tangible things you can personally do to ensure all members of the church are connected to one another?

6. If you have a disability ministry in your church, assess how involved you are in it. Do you see it as a "niche" ministry for specially gifted Christians, or a calling for all believers?

FOR CHURCH ASSESSMENT

1. Does your church have a vibrant ministry to individuals and families touched by disability? If not, do you know why not?

2. If your church has a disability ministry, assess its effectiveness. Is it a core ministry to the church, or a "fringe" ministry? Does the congregation embrace the work of ministry to those touched by disability, or privately oppose it?

3. Think about specific ways your church is working to allow people with all sorts of disabilities to be included in all ministry aspects. Do visitors who have children with disabilities know that their children will be fully included? How about in the youth ministry?

4. While there are laws that require buildings to be accessible (and this applies to your church buildings), take stock of all the ways your church is not accessible. This includes all of the programs and ministries of the church as well as its facilities.

5. Consider ways your church can offer rest and respite to parents who are constantly caring for their family members touched by disability. If your church is already offering respite care, what can be done to reach more people in the disability community? How can more members of your congregation get involved?

6. People with disability need to be fully included in your church. That also means they need their gifts and talents and interests utilized as members of the body of Christ. How is your church promoting this sort of involvement and activity for those who are suffering?

For Group Discussion

1. Why do human beings often choose independence and isolation rather than interdependence and relationships?

2. Why does God's Word teach us that the church is a family?

3. How does our adoption in Christ connect us to disability ministry?

4. Is it possible for Christians in the church to truly act as a family? Why or why not?

5. How is a church which is not actively involved in disability ministry operating as an unhealthy, dysfunctional family?

6. What does the childlike lesson of "sharing" have to do with disability ministry?

7. How can your church provide accessibility *and* inclusion to those suffering with disabilities?

8. What makes a "buddy system" so important for the church to act as a functional family?

9. How is respite care a display of the church acting as a family?

CHAPTER 6

THE CHURCH AS A DISCIPLESHIP CULTURE

Biblical Counseling in the Church

For people who are suffering, the local church acting as a spiritual hospital is a welcome sight. The hospitality and the care from the congregation will go a long way in bringing healing to body, mind, and soul. When the church acts as a healthy, inclusive, and accessible family, our brothers and sisters with diseases, disabilities, and disorders will be right at home. All Christians are welcome into the family of God! Yet, a clear reading of Scripture will not allow the church to be only two-dimensional, merely giving attention to mercy ministry or the fellowship of the brethren. The church is called by God to be a community of disciples, passionate lovers of Christ, who are growing in Christlikeness and being used by Christ to make disciples. This picture is given most concretely in Jesus' great commission to the apostles of the early church: "Go therefore and make disciples of all nations, baptizing them in the name of the Father and of the Son and of the Holy Spirit, teaching them to observe all that I have commanded you. And behold, I am with you always, to the end of the age" (Matthew 28:19-20). For all who suffer with disease, disability, and disorder, the local church must be a culture of intentional daily and mutual discipleship.[52]

The Picture of a Discipling Church
A Culture of Change

How many of your church members wake up Sunday morning, put on their Sunday best, and think to themselves: "I can't wait to go to church today so I can change!"? What if I changed the question to: "How many of your church members know they need to change in the first place?" Certainly, those who most clearly see their sins, or recognize an area of weakness, understand their need for change. The reality is that even when we have been brought from death to life by the Spirit, and have had our status changed to a justified, redeemed, adopted child of God in Christ, we still have much to change. In order to do that most effectively, we must not just be dependent on self. We need to be immersed into a culture that enables us to change to be more like Christ. And that primary culture is found in the local church.

Typically, Christians are well aware of how the culture of this dark world changes people. Parents are rightly concerned about the impact of a pagan culture when their children become teens or college students. They pray that their childlike faith in Christ will not somehow be changed as the world seeks to conform them to itself. When we pay attention to our own lives, we can often see the impact of how the world changes our thought processes, or language, and our affections with what it has to offer. So there should be no argument that a shared culture is a culture of change. It seeks to put us into its mold. It seeks to ensure that everyone thinks the same. What happens when a young Christian goes out to Hollywood to become an actor or actress? If he or she is to remain unchanged by that culture, another culture will have to be more dominant. The same goes for our students who are off on a secular college campus. And the best culture of change occurs in a discipling church.

Within the context of a church with a discipleship culture, suffering itself will change us. Using the image of the fiery furnace to describe the change suffering brings, Keller states:

> *We have said suffering is like a furnace—like painful, searing heat that creates purity and beauty. And now we can see one of the ways it does this. Suffering puts its*

fingers on good things that have become too important to us.
We must respond to suffering not ordinarily by jettisoning
those loved things but by turning to God and loving Him
more, and by putting our roots down deeper into him.[53]

This is the ongoing change that disciples who are suffering
need. It's not just about fixing the problem (if it can even be
fixed in the first place), but, rather, replacing the lesser loves in
our hearts with the greater ones. Suffering has a way of putting
back in order what has been disordered. And for all of us, our
love for God demands the most change. And, thankfully, it
is ultimately the transforming love of God that changes us
(1 John 3:1).

To be clear, a church that creates a culture of change
does not equate to a church that is unaccepting, intolerant,
and judgmental toward sufferers. Unfortunately, these two
operational stances are often conflated by those inside and
outside the church. When believers assert that homosexuality
is sinful and requires biblical change, we can be perceived as
being unloving, as well as ignorant to the science that asserts
homosexuality is genetic. When the church seeks to address the
heart issues involved in substance abuse, again we can be seen
as intolerant and rejecting of addicts. When attempts are made
to understand any disorder as also being a spiritual problem,
there will be some who believe this is a lack of grace and mercy.
So while the church must always lead with compassion for
sufferers, this does not preclude us from also holding out the
hope of biblical change, where change is possible and necessary!

As we discussed in the first section of this book, change often
looks different for each one of the 3-Ds. Most individuals with
diseases are in search of a cure. People with disabilities are often
forced to see change in small increments, but also may only
experience debilitating change over time. Many of our mental,
emotional, and relational disorders bring with them a biblical
hope of change. Yet, as believers, change is not just connected
to whether a problem is a disease, disability, or disorder—it is
connected to the person involved. By the transforming work of
the Spirit and the Word, all sufferers can and will be changed.
We are changed when we are justified. We are changed in the
process of sanctification. And we will one day enjoy the change

of glorified bodies! Transformative change is the essence of our discipleship. Therefore, the healthy church is all about Christian growth and change.[54]

A CULTURE OF HELPING RELATIONSHIPS

Love one another (John 13:34). Honor one another above yourselves (Romans 12:10). Accept one another (Romans 15:7). Instruct one another (Romans 15:14). Have equal concern for one another (1 Corinthians 12:25). Serve one another (Galatians 5:13). Bear one another's burdens (Galatians 6:2). Be kind and compassionate to one another (Ephesians 4:32). Teach and admonish one another (Colossians 3:16). Encourage one another (1 Thessalonians 4:18). Pray for one another (James 5:16). What do these and a dozen more New Testament commands have in common? They are works of grace that believers are called to do for and with "one another" in a discipleship culture. These commands push us past our familial relationships into helping relationships—with an eye to discipling one another. Mark Dever and Paul Alexander put it this way:

> *A healthy by-product of non-staff members discipling other members is that it promotes a growing culture of distinctively Christian community, in which people are loving one another not simply as the world loves, but as followers of Christ who are together seeking to understand and live out the implication of His Word for their lives.*[55]

Garrett Higbee also sees the importance of all Christians being part of a helping culture for those who are suffering: "But I believe that the value of teaching our people to speak the truth in love to one another at every level of the body of believers is the missing ingredient today."[56]

There are certainly individuals who are gifted in a unique way to listen, evaluate, confront, and educate people with diseases, disabilities, and disorders. God has called particular Christians to be regularly laboring as biblical counselors, in full- or part-time gospel ministry. There is also necessary knowledge and skillsets required, which includes advanced training and possibly even a graduate degree. So, just as we need trained and ordained ministers of the gospel to shepherd the flock, local congregations need trained, competent, and gifted biblical counselors as well. But those pastors and ministry leaders should be involved in leading people to help one another. As Jeremy Pierre and Deepak Reju exhort: "Basically, pastor, if you want help with your counseling, start by building a culture of discipleship in your church. If you are building a people committed to one another's spiritual good, they will be more interested in counseling as a tool that can help toward that end."[57]

So, as the "one anothering" verses in the New Testament epistles demonstrate, there is a certain responsibility that Christians have for each other that should not be just left to "the professionals." All Christians are to be actively ministering to those most closely connected to them. To be able to love, serve, admonish, teach, encourage, and bear burdens—all of these require a real helping relationship. So, people carrying a particular "burden" often need an abundance of biblical counselors all around them. True, helpful, accountability is often a missing element in our churches, and this presents a significant obstacle to the process of biblical change. Christians in the local church must become more connected to their "informal" work as biblical counselors. All Christians are to be at the ready to give wise counsel, biblical advice, and the application of sound doctrine to those in need.

A CULTURE OF KNOWLEDGE AND WISDOM

One of my favorite word-origin stories is the development of the term "educate." From the Latin root "educare," which means "to lead out," the term has the strong sense of one person leading another person "out."[58] The question is: out of "where" or "what?" The best answer to that question is that "to educate" another person is to lead him or her out of *ignorance*! Having weak and sinful minds, we all need to be "educated" out of our lack of knowledge, into a place of greater knowledge. To put it in terms found all through Proverbs, we require more and more knowledge in order to move from folly to wisdom (Proverbs 10:14). Becoming more educated in the biblical sense of the word is not just becoming more knowledgeable, but wisely living out that increased knowledge. So a discipleship culture is grounded in knowledge and wisdom, seeking to lead people *out of* ignorance *into* the truth.

Think about how the matter of knowledge and wisdom is essential for all sufferers, especially those with a mental and emotional disorder. For example, Pam, a woman in your congregation who struggles with anxiety, may lack knowledge in the following areas:

- An understanding that anxiety is often aroused when we are trying to control what we can't control;
- A knowledge of what God's Word says about anxiety;
- A right knowledge of God, His character, His power, and His works;
- A right knowledge of self, others, and her responses;
- An understanding of the interaction of her thoughts, attitudes, and actions;
- A right view of grace, change, and the work and fruit of the Spirit;
- An understanding of how her bodily health may be involved.

In order for biblical change for a disorder to occur, knowledge of the truth is required—knowledge that grows out of the grace of God and faith in Jesus Christ. Knowledge and understanding are foundational for wisdom to be operative in our lives. Therefore, a person with a problem of any kind must be led out of a certain amount of ignorance. To put it in a more Christ-centered way, the truth has to set him or her free (John 8:32).

So while the context of discipleship is helping relationships, the content of discipleship is Christ-centered knowledge and wisdom. Pierre and Reju define it this way: "Discipleship... means to love one another by speaking and living according to God's Word together."[59] We impart the knowledge of God and his Word to those who are suffering out of love for God and one another. Yet that knowledge must be more than "academic" in nature. A person growing in knowledge and wisdom is not someone really smart, knows his Bible trivia, or is really skilled in a particular knowledge domain. Rather, a gospel-driven knowledge promotes godly wisdom—with the end goal of transformation. Biblical knowledge must lead to wise living, as Paul modeled to the church at Philippi: "What you have learned and received and heard and seen in me—practice these things, and the God of peace will be with you" (Philippians 4:9).

A Culture of Maturity and Unity

Is your church unintentionally creating more of a day-care culture rather than a discipling culture? In other words, are your church members just sort of dropping in for a while, "playing" at church, seeking to be entertained, whining when things aren't going their way, and then returning to their real home? No offense to quality day-care centers out there, but in most of them, there is no real system in place for producing mature children—but simply a focus on caring for them until their parents pick them up. Churches can act like that's all that is to be expected as well, and then end up seeing most of their members remaining immature. Instead, we should make clear in our churches that much more is expected from all believers. Here's how Pierre and Reju put it:

> *We should strive to make church a place where being anonymous or nominal is difficult to pull off. We want the healthy pressure of the preached Word and Christian relationships to press in on the believer's life. In other words, your people should know that active discipleship is an expectation of your church.*[60]

Without this expectation, how can we think that more than just the minority of church members to grow in maturity?

One of the most powerful descriptions of the goal of all our discipleship is found in Ephesians 4. As was mentioned earlier, Paul speaks of how the church has been given great gifts by King Jesus for the equipping of the saints, to do the work of the ministry. Then we see the goal of this discipleship process emerge:

> *And he gave the apostles, the prophets, the evangelists, the shepherds and teachers, to equip the saints for the work of ministry, for building up*

> *the body of Christ, until we all attain to the unity of*
> *the faith and of the knowledge of the Son of God, to*
> *mature manhood, to the measure of the stature of*
> *the fullness of Christ, so that we may no longer be*
> *children, tossed to and fro by the waves and carried*
> *about by every wind of doctrine, by human cunning,*
> *by craftiness in deceitful schemes. Rather, speaking*
> *the truth in love, we are to grow up in every way into*
> *him who is the head, into Christ, from whom the*
> *whole body, joined and held together by every joint*
> *with which it is equipped, when each part is working*
> *properly, makes the body grow so that it builds itself*
> *up in love.*
>
> *(Ephesians 4:11-16)*

Over and over again, Paul emphasizes one of the goals of discipleship: "mature manhood," "no longer children," "grow up in every way," and "makes the body grow." Suffering with diseases, disabilities, and disorders certainly gives us the opportunity to grow and mature. Yet, if we are not given biblical truth and wisdom, then suffering can just as easily keep us (or make us more) immature. We can either be tossed to and fro by every wind of doctrine, or gain spiritual health that will make us strong and steady in the storms of life.

Intertwined with the primary goal of maturity, unity is intended to be a result of a discipling culture as well. In one sense, a goal of unity of believers brings us back to the church-as-family, connected to each other as brothers and sisters in Christ. Yet Paul refers to this sort of closeness as the "unity of faith and of the knowledge of the Son of God." How does that relate to our suffering? It means that whether we have a disease, disability, or disorder, the way we become unified with one another is directly related to our faith. To put it in the negative, if our present suffering is pulling us away from the faith and knowledge of the Son of God, then we will also be less unified with other believers. Positively speaking, growing in grace will give us the same heart and mind as other faithful disciples of Christ. So, a culture of discipleship must also be one that pursues unity of believers who are maturing in Christ.

A CULTURE OF DISCIPLINE

We misunderstand what a discipling culture looks like if we don't include the biblical process of church discipline. After all, the terms "disciple" and "discipline" derive from the same root. Most Christian adults have little trouble understanding why parents are commanded to discipline their children. No one really enjoys being in a home where children are unruly, disrespectful, foolish, and rebellious due to the fact that they are undisciplined! But transferring that concept to the church can be a challenge at times. We may give lip service to the need for church discipline to occur, but resistant when it is actually attempted. Unfortunately, many Christians, and even church leaders, believe that the disciplining accountability of church members to elders in a local congregation is an archaic notion. And that has left many of our congregations without the full opportunity to become a discipling culture. It will keep us from becoming what Paul teaches Titus to be: "hospitable, a lover of good, self-controlled, upright, holy, and *disciplined*" (Titus 1:8).

Even if we are committed to the biblical notion of church discipline, what does that have to do with people who are suffering? After all, discipline is for rebellious sinners, doing publicly wicked things, right? Yes and no. Certainly, what we commonly think of as "negative" discipline is required for public sin that is threatening the peace and purity of the church. Additionally, the elders of the church are required by God's Word to discipline those who are unwilling to see their sin, repent, and grow in holiness (Matthew 18:15-17). So, if a church member is suffering purely from his own sinful choices, then church discipline may be required. This does not mean biblical care and counseling won't also be offered; yet, the discipline of the church may have to help the process along. This negative discipline, brought to bear in love, can move a person to deal with the problems in his or her life.

But we would be remiss if we only think of discipline as some sort of negative, condemning, punitive event. The writer to the Hebrew Christians describes it much more positively: "For the Lord disciplines the one he loves, and chastises every son whom he receives . . . God is treating you as sons . . ." (Hebrews 12:6-7). Discipline is meant to be a loving process that has a positive result in the lives of believers, even those who are suffering. As the writer of Hebrews continues: "For the moment all discipline seems painful rather than pleasant, but later it yields the peaceful fruit of righteousness to those who have been trained by it" (Hebrews 12:11). Church discipline is a positive process, not allowing people to stay isolated and alone in their individual, marital, or familial disorders. When a particular problem gets to a place where more people are needed to provide help, then church discipline provides the avenue. When biblical confrontation is needed because of sin that has become attached to the disorder, then church discipline is potentially positive and redemptive. Far from being a way of just kicking bad people out of the church, it is a demonstration of the accountability of believers joined together in Christ. When a church refuses to practice biblical church discipline, it only enables people to become even more isolated, independent, and stuck in their suffering.

The Practice of Biblical Counseling in the Church

When the local church embraces its biblical responsibility to be a discipleship culture, then every one of its ministries will become more focused on promoting the growth of the followers of Jesus. Yet, just as it was asserted that the church cannot truly be operating as a family without a disability ministry, it will also be deficient without a dedicated biblical counseling ministry. People who suffer with diseases, disabilities, and disorders require Christ-centered, gospel-driven counseling as they wrestle with many of the problems that fall in those categories. This final section will seek to briefly describe the practice of biblical counseling in the church, specifically related to how it can help with all of the 3-Ds of suffering. Fundamentally, it must be understood as fully connected to the discipleship occurring throughout the church, as is well summarized by Robert Kellemen: "We have wrongly defined biblical counseling so that it is about solving problems. We've made it a subset of discipleship focused on reactive work with persons struggling with sin. Instead, we should think of biblical counseling as synonymous with comprehensive personal discipleship."[61]

PREACHING AND TEACHING

Why do Christian pastors preach, week in and week out, in pulpits all over the world? Certainly, they preach in order to glorify God, and lift high the gospel of grace found in Jesus Christ alone. But why does God call preachers to preach? What is his ultimate purpose for preaching? Remember the words of Paul to the Church at Rome: "For I am not ashamed of the gospel, for it is the power of God for salvation to everyone who believes, to the Jew first and also to the Greek" (Romans 1:16). Men are called by God to preach the gospel with the clear objective of people coming to saving faith in Jesus Christ. Proclaiming the Word of God with the power of the Spirit produces genuine heart transformation. So, a preacher is not fulfilling his calling by God if he is not preaching with the purpose of seeing real heart change in his people.

So, our churches must be filled with preachers who are powerfully expositing the Word of God in all boldness, trusting in the Spirit to do his work in the lives of people. Ministers of the Word should apply God's Word to all the situations of life, instructing the congregation in godliness and righteousness. If we rightly see the central place of the Bible in our Christian lives, we should see how it also deals with all of our diseases, disabilities, and disorders in this life. God's Word speaks to problems in marriage and family life, as well as to our self, anxiety, anger, depressive, and addictive disorders. It instructs us how we are to respond to our disabilities and diseases. Therefore, in one sense, a pastor who preaches a biblically sound and comprehensive gospel will be practicing biblical counseling from the pulpit! This is especially true if we see preaching as not just a vehicle of evangelism, but also of Christian discipleship. William Goode makes this point as well:

> *Counselees need the help of all church ministries: they need the pulpit ministry to teach and motivate growth and change, the love of the collective membership to assist and encourage, the fellowship of the church body for interaction and relationships, the authority of the body for church discipline, and the examples of leaders who are growing and changing.*[62]

The same should be true for the teaching that goes on in a typical local congregation. Many churches have either Sunday school classes for all ages or discipleship groups which teach and apply the Scriptures. Added to these core activities are small-group Bible studies, mid-week discipleship classes, youth groups, catechism classes, community groups, and the list goes on. In various ways, we teach individuals of all ages the truth that is in Jesus Christ, as found in the Word of God. Sound doctrine is to be learned in order to grow in Christ, and to be witnesses of Jesus Christ to a dying world. Yet again, the application of a strong biblical theology must be brought to bear upon all of our suffering. Our Bible and theological studies should seek to reach those who are struggling with disease, disability, and disorder. This would also include the teaching of special series each year pertaining to how to handle all sorts of problems, according to God's Word and gospel wisdom.

Unfortunately, when it comes to what are commonly called "mental illnesses" by our modern culture, it appears that churches may be inadequately addressing certain suffering issues, especially in our preaching and teaching ministries. According to recent research on the topic of mental illness in Protestant churches, 66 percent of pastors speak to their church once a year or less on mental illness related subjects. Compare that to the 59 percent of those with mental and emotional disorders who want their church to talk about them much more openly, and you have missed opportunities for biblical counseling from the pulpit.[63] If those numbers are legitimate, our church leaders should not just assume that we are showing enough concern for those who are suffering when our most significant public proclamation of the Word is silent. What are we saying about God's Word being sufficient to deal with all of the problems of life if we are not actually preaching that truth from the pulpit?

Formal and Informal

In modern times, we are used to thinking about counseling as only what occurs in an office between a trained professional and a counselee. When your friend says, "I need counseling," you don't typically respond, "How can I help you?" Instead, you will probably share the contact information of a trusted counselor so he can make an appointment. While formal biblical counseling should always be available in the church, it will never be enough to deal with all of the suffering that exists in the congregation. Even if your church has several pastors or staff members who are trained biblical counselors, this will be a very inefficient system. Writing on this subject, Higbee envisions a much better process, one with:

> *A combination of informal and formal counsel where discipleship and biblical counseling are on the same continuum...it intentionally tries to avoid structuring biblical counseling as a solo ministry...instead is working in partnership with each discipleship avenue in the local church....* [64]

A church that has a discipleship culture will see more and more people offering biblical counseling to one another, in both formal and informal settings.

FORMAL COUNSELING

First, the local church, whether small or large, should strive to provide formalized biblical counseling to all who desire it. As a biblical counselor in my church, I often joke with members of our congregation that, sooner or later, everyone will make a visit to my office (or to the office of one of the other pastors). I know, that sounds like I'm the high school vice principal, and all our members will get into trouble at some point. Or, people may understand me to be saying that I believe that we will all develop some sort of disorder if we live long enough. That actually may be closer to the truth of my halfway serious jesting. In reality, I'm typically just trying to dispel the myth that only a very few people in the church have problems, while most other people are just fine and dandy. The truth is that Christians will find their lives out of order at times, experiencing difficult depression, anxiety, bitterness, addiction, marriage problems, and other issues. People may never want to formally visit the office of the biblical counselor, but it may be necessary in order to implement biblical change.

So, if the members of our congregation are willing to receive biblical counseling in the local church, what must be offered by pastors, elders and ministry leaders? First, individuals and couples who are suffering need our *time*. While preaching and teaching are activities that make the most use of time (one hour per dozens or hundreds of people), counseling requires more time for far fewer people (one hour per person). But that's exactly what our members who are hurting the most need! They need time to tell their story. They require time for the story to be heard and understood. They need time to have gospel conversations. They must be given time to be accountable for applying solutions to the problems. Biblical counseling is not just a brief time of dispensing pious advice or a quick Scripture verse and a prayer. People need time with Christians who will effectively walk with them through their stubborn disorders.

A person who is suffering also needs *compassion*. One of my favorite counseling professors regularly taught us that counseling is 20 percent skill and 80 percent compassion. While probably not totally accurate, his point was well taken. If our Lord Jesus Christ was described many times as being "moved by compassion" (Matthew 9:36, 14:14) when he saw hurting people, then so must his people be. Let's face it, people who are hurting, struggling, and caught in a disorder can tell if another person cares or not. Compassion isn't something that can be faked—at least not for long. It is a heart attitude of mercy that wells up from deep within us when we truly know what God has done for us in Jesus Christ. It is the true merger of sympathy and empathy which pours out into a passionate desire for people to experience freedom in Christ. Compassion produces understanding coupled with wisdom, directed to solution for the glory of God and the good of another.

A third essential for people who are suffering need are biblical counselors who are *skilled* in the art and craft of counseling. Now there will always be debate by Christians over what constitutes the proper training and education in order for someone to become skillful as a counselor. What is typically agreed upon is that counselors need to be trained listeners and communicators, and have a proper understanding of the human being. Biblical counselors would also prioritize a right understanding of God in order to have essential expertise regarding the human being, his problems, and solutions to those problems. In other words, while practical counseling skills are mandatory, so is sound theology and doctrine. It's not that people need professionals in order to change, but skilled and gifted counselors certainly help the process greatly. Local churches should have as many pastors, elders, and ministry leaders trained in biblical counseling as possible.

INFORMAL COUNSELING

In his book on equipping counselors in the church, Kellemen makes this sweeping assertion: "Biblical counseling is the calling of all of God's people all of the time because we are striving to grow in Christ all of the time."[65] What does this mean? Again, it does not negate that only particular Christians are gifted, called, and skilled to give their time and compassion in the practice of biblical counseling. It simply recognizes two truths: (1) All Christians counsel others by their examples, words, and entire lives all the time; and (2) All Christians who are committed to living by biblical truth are compelled to be a witness of that truth to others. The reality is that people in the church and outside of the truth are watching us all the time. They will even regularly ask for our advice, our input, and our counsel, if we make ourselves available. All Christians who are growing as Jesus' disciples must be ready to give an answer for their hope and for the basic problems that suffering people face all the time (1 Peter 3:15).

When a church is maintaining a discipleship culture, it is acting as a cooperative learning center (informal counseling), not just a (formal) tutoring clinic. Just as Christians learn side by side in the Sunday school classroom or Bible study group, we also must deal with our problems side by side. We are not only to help one another in relationships, but also to learn from one another. This truth is somewhat revealed to us by the success of the modern self-help group. How much better it is to hear that some other church members have experienced the same disorder or difficulty in their lives. It is both reassuring ("I'm not the only one!") and an opportunity for relationship ("Will you walk with me through this?"). Viewing the church as a sort of discipleship learning lab means that we are all in this together. Whatever our personal experiences, we need the entire body of Christ, with all of its corporate expertise, in order to provide accountability leading to biblical change.

Focus on Marriage and Family

Do you remember the "prayer chain" illustration from the introduction to the first chapter? How often do you see requests in your church bulletin like: "Pray for my marriage, as I consider separating from my husband," or, "Please pray for the challenges we are having disciplining our angry son"? Yet we know that the marriages and families in our churches are suffering, often in silence. There are numerous reasons why the divorce rates of evangelical Christians are so high, and there are many reasons for the fact that Christian families experience their share of family problems. Just as an act of mercy alone, our biblical counseling efforts should always be ramping up to focus on our marriages and families. Not only do we need to help those who are hurting in our congregation for their own sake, but for the sake of the overall well-being of the kingdom of God. When Christian marriages and families crumble, what is the impact in the wider world? Here again, a true discipleship culture needs to make changes in marriage and family life, or we will succumb to the unhealthy, broken culture of this world.

So this reminds us that when a church is paying attention to the diseases, disabilities, and disorders present in the congregation, relational problems will always accompany them. Certainly, mental and emotional problems can produce marriage and family issues; yet, many of our individual problems end up manifesting first within a relationship. While it is vital for Claire to seek help for her chronic depression, what if it is mainly the result of a difficult marriage? While counseling Duke, a twelve-year-old boy, for acting out at school, you discover his rebellion is being provoked by his fears that his parents are about to get a divorce. What do we focus on in this case? In many ways, most of our disorders are either revealed in marriage and family life, or are the consequence of those relationships. As Christians who stand for healthy biblical marriage and families, our attention should always be on the state of our closest of human relationships.

What about the parent-child relationships in your midst? If you took a survey of the mothers and fathers in your congregation, what would be reported regarding where they seek counsel when they lack knowledge and wisdom in how to deal with their children? Maybe they ask their pediatrician or a child psychologist. Or, there is always the Internet. And of course, there are shelves and shelves of self-help books in most bookstores devoted to parenting. But, how many in your congregation actually go to their pastor, a church ministry leader, an elder, or even a friend, for wise counsel? How many of them even know that any of those helpers are actually available? While there is certainly help to be found "out there," there is absolutely no reason for Christians to not be equipped and available in the church where they may offer parenting counseling. After all, we have access to God's Word, to the Holy Spirit, and to heavenly wisdom! If we are serious about discipleship in the church, then marriage and parenting must be high on the list of our biblical counseling priorities.

COUNSELING DISEASE

In 2006, on the eve of his own cancer surgery, John Piper wrote a brilliant article, which later became a book, entitled: "Don't Waste your Cancer."[66] In it, he gives ten heart-changing points of biblical counsel that, over this last decade, continue to encourage and motivate people with cancer as well as other diseases. As a pastor who is committed to biblical counseling in the local church, Piper also gave us a model of how to counsel all people with diseases. Instead of simply focusing on their physical and material needs, the church is also called to counsel people biblically through their suffering. They need to be confronted lovingly and truthfully from God's Word. We tend to expect people with all sorts of sickness and disease to struggle with anger, anxiety, depression, and even addiction; but, do we proactively intervene in these issues? Or, do we just accept that emotional and mental disorders are the unavoidable consequence of difficult diseases? A healthy biblical counseling ministry seeks out people struggling with disease to offer them spiritual counsel and hope.

Aaron was diagnosed with a non-operable brain tumor ten years ago. He has been married for twelve years, and now has five young children. Most members of your church think that all is well with this young couple because, after all, Aaron is still alive, able to work, and seems happy. Yet, when a pastor finally visits with Aaron and Brenda, he hears a much different story. Due to the long-term chemotherapy and radiation treatment that was required, Aaron has lost all of his ability to show affection or display much emotion at all. This has not gone over very well with a young wife who craves a normal amount of husbandly attention and affection. Add to this Aaron's fatigue because of the ongoing treatments and his loss of memory, and you have the perfect storm of marital issues. Since the focus has been primarily on the disease, the ensuing marital disorders have not been addressed well. Now, with these issues much more deeply engrained, regular formal biblical counseling is required, as well as informal accountability from other believers.

Patsy has suffered with an undiagnosed chronic illness for just over three years. She experiences severe migraine headaches nearly every day, as well as dizziness, fatigue, and other sensory issues. Patsy's husband, Lou, has spent much time and money taking her to medical experts from coast to coast. Recently, Patsy has become more and more depressed, isolating herself from her closest friends. Early in the course of her condition, she regularly called on the church elders to pray for her. She was also extremely faithful in church attendance and was deeply involved in the women's ministry. But as of now, she hasn't been in church for six months and refuses to receive any pastoral visitation or congregational care. Formal biblical counseling has been rejected, since she believes that nothing can be done for her disease, which has ultimately become a disability. How does the church help here? In addition to faithful prayer, the persistent, informal counseling of brothers and sisters in Christ will be required!

When we have a three-dimensional view of suffering in the church, we see the vital connection between hospital-like congregational care and discipleship-based biblical counseling. When disease strikes, we typically mobilize the members of the church to pray, serve, and care—addressing all immediate needs. But if a disease progresses, becomes chronic, or is deemed to be incurable, there will end up being opportunities to offer informal and formal biblical counseling. Some members of your church may reach out for counseling on their own; others will need to be pursued. But the most important thing is that we don't neglect to focus on the person (and the connected family) because we are only preoccupied with the disease.

COUNSELING DISABILITY

In a similar way, it is easy for our congregation to focus so much on familial accessibility and inclusion that we don't consider the counseling needs of those touched by disability. As was discussed previously, churches can become content with making sure there are wheelchair spots in the sanctuary, listening devices available in the foyer, and maybe even a sign language expert ready to communicate. Yet, people touched with disabilities also need to receive biblical counseling for their mental, emotional, spiritual, and relational problems as well. When we are not focused on discipling and offering biblical counseling to individuals with disabilities, we are communicating that they are somewhat less than human—lacking normal human life struggles. A person with a physical disability just becomes someone who needs help with his or her physical body. An individual with an intellectual disability is perceived to only require help to learn or to communicate. When the disability appears to be the sole issue to address, we will miss the opportunity to solve the problems of the heart, mind, and soul. Whatever the case, we are remiss to not pursue the counseling needs of individuals suffering with disabilities, as well as the needs of their caregivers.

Ethan is a twenty-seven-year-old who has been diagnosed with a disability on the autism spectrum. Even though he is extremely intelligent, he cannot drive a car or live on his own. Ethan has watched all of his high school and college friends get married and start families, which doesn't seem possible for him. He struggles just to have an hourly job in the food industry. Ethan's parents talk with you about his angry outbursts and his bouts of depression. Cara, an older woman who has been confined to a wheelchair most of her life, also struggles with anger and anxiety. With her physical limitations, as well as her difficulty communicating, most people don't give her much of a hearing. Yet Cara is desperate for some biblical counsel regarding her relationship with her mother. She is tired of being treated like a child! How do we make sure Ethan and Cara have opportunities to receive biblical counseling?

Kelvin had a motorcycle accident as a young man, and has been suffering with quadriplegia ever since. Three years ago, he became a Christian and also married his high school sweetheart.

His wife, Elaine, has been confiding with the ladies in her Bible study about the fatigue she often feels in caretaking—and the guilt and shame it produces. She wants to receive biblical marital counseling, but Kelvin isn't interested. He's afraid that the pastor will just point out what a terrible husband he is, or be afraid to address his intimacy issues. Then there is the Andersen family. Two of their three boys are on the autistic spectrum. Their family life is chaotic, to say the least. They would like to talk to their pastor, but are worried he may just point out what terrible parents they are. After all, how much of the problem with their boys is autism, and how much is sin? Then, there's the difficult question of church membership as well.

When becoming too focused on the impairment, we may not even consider that there are individuals touched by disability who just need to talk. They need someone who will listen to their story, just as all people do when we experience great suffering. In this way, biblical counseling is also connected to the church-as-family. It provides brotherly love and affection to someone in need. It gives an opportunity for an individual with a disability to break out of isolation, when finding friends in the church is difficult. At its core, biblical counseling is relational, seeking to restore people to Christ and to his church. And, as biblical counseling is also connected to the discipleship culture of the church, it is an entrance way to further allow people with disabilities to learn to be a part of the family of God. It is past time for our biblical counseling ministries to pay greater attention to people touched by disability and the unique mental, emotional, and relational disorders that proceed from their situation.

For Personal Reflection

1. Think again about your own present suffering. Is it causing you to change, maturing more in Christ? Or does it feel like it's restricting your growth in Christ?

2. Consider the periods of time in your life where you grew the most as a believer. Was it during times of suffering, or when everything appeared to be easy and calm?

3. Who is discipling you right now? Think back to all the people who have contributed to your coming to Christ and to your spiritual growth. Did you actively seek a relationship with Christians who could help you, or did they "just happen" to come into your life?

4. Make a list of the areas where you lack wisdom. Then, seek wisdom from a godly friend or a biblical counselor! Also, pray for wisdom, as Scripture teaches us. We often don't have wisdom because we don't ask.

5. In what ways do you see yourself as a mature Christian? In some ways, we often don't feel like we will ever be mature—especially in particular areas. Think about how God defines Christian maturity and use that as your ultimate standard.

6. Assess the ways that you are being disciplined right now, especially in your current suffering. While no discipline is pleasant and enjoyable, are you seeking for the Lord to discipline you in all possible ways? Or are you resisting his hand of discipline?

For Church Assessment

1. Evaluate the ministry of biblical counseling in your church. Do your pastors offer biblical counseling to church members? How about non-members? Are the elders involved or other staff members? Have ministry leaders been trained in biblical counseling?

2. Think about the regular preaching in the church. Is there application given to our emotional, mental, spiritual, and relational disorders?

3. How much informal biblical counseling is going on in your church, from member to member? Is your congregation being regularly trained to counsel one another in order to see change in people's disorders?

4. Does your church view counseling as a ministry of a church or more of a professional activity best left for other institutions? More specifically, what are the beliefs of your ministry leaders, and what is the possible resistance to biblical counseling in the church?

5. Think through your church directory. Do you know the marriages that are struggling and in need of biblical counseling? What about parenting issues? What are ministry opportunities for your church to build up your marriages and families?

6. Consider how people struggling with a disease or a disability in your church also need biblical counseling. Why do we tend to only think about healing for a disease or accessibility for a disability, rather than seeing people as needing wise counsel as they experience their particular form of suffering?

7. In what ways does your church need to connect the vital ministries of disability ministry and biblical counseling ministry?

FOR GROUP DISCUSSION

1. How is the local church a "discipleship culture?"

2. Why is discipleship all about change?

3. How do you see people in your church counseling one another?

4. How are knowledge and wisdom essential for true discipleship?

5. What does maturity and unity look like in the church?

6. How is the preaching of the gospel connected to biblical counseling?

7. How are all Christians in a local church to do the work of biblical counseling?

8. How is the work of biblical counseling connected to the fuller life of the local church?

9. Why does biblical counseling require relational accountability?

10. How is biblical counseling even necessary for diseases and disabilities? Specifically, why do churches struggle to connect biblical counseling to disability ministry?

CONCLUDING THOUGHTS

There aren't too many teenagers in your church who spend their afternoons thinking: "One day, I'm going to have a diving accident and spend the rest of my life in a wheelchair." Even though statistics show that nearly 40 percent of men and women will develop some type of cancer at some point in their lives, ten out of ten members in your church probably think that they aren't part of that four. And, most churchgoers likely think that significant disorders such as debilitating anxiety, depression, and addictions will only affect someone much weaker in their midst. But the reality is that, at some point in our lives, and maybe at many points in our lives, we will suffer with a disease, disability, or a disorder. That isn't just some voice of pessimism or a type of anti-Christian fatalism. It is the recognition that we are people living in a fallen world who will suffer from internal and external causes, contributors, and consequences. And, as believers in Jesus Christ, we are the only ones who can embrace this truth as well as its solution.

So, when you find yourself in one or more of the many, many types of the problems within the 3-Ds, what will be your attitude regarding your local church? In other words, how will you operate among God's people then? Will you call upon the church to act as God's Word prescribes—as your hospital, your family, and your discipleship culture? Or will you possibly descend into despair as you observe the church not living up to its calling well? Or even worse, will you simply look for help only from anything and everyone else outside the church, believing your church family to be totally ineffective for you? My hope is that you will not only give your church an opportunity to function in God-glorifying ways, but you will allow fellow believers to participate and help in your suffering. That will require a growing faith in Christ as well as a willingness to be vulnerable and take risks. Whatever happens, it will be worth it—as God will cause you to grow in grace.

There will also be times where you find yourself on the "helper" side of things in your church, as a pastor, elder, ministry leader, or layperson. Will you be quick to respond to brothers or sisters in Christ who present with diseases, disabilities, or disorders? Or will you keep your distance, assuming someone else—anyone else—is more capable of helping? It's certainly tempting to steer clear of all people in most of the categories of human suffering, but it is really not an option for you as a professing follower of Jesus Christ. As he entered into the suffering of his people, all who bear his name must do the same. The presence of people with diseases, disabilities, and disorders provides a great welcome mat to participate in the sufferings of Christ as we suffer with his people. Just always remember that you are not called to be the great rescuer or the savior, but simply to be a tool in the Suffering Servant's hands.

Well, where do we go from here? Hopefully, thinking more deeply about the 3-Ds of suffering, and their connection to the church, is more than an academic exercise. After all, Paul wrote to the church at Corinth the reality that, ". . . knowledge puffs up, but love builds up." (1 Corinthians 8:1). Having a greater understanding of human suffering, we must always be compelled to a deeper love for God and others. So, there are plenty of practical steps and application for the church to learn as it grows in its work as a hospital, a family, and a discipleship culture. Connecting the ministries of congregational care, disability ministry, and biblical counseling is necessary as we forge a path forward as faithful churches of Jesus Christ. Where else should people with diseases, disabilities, and disorders go where they can be understood, welcomed, loved, and discipled, than to the grace-filled, gospel-driven body of Christ?

ENDNOTES

1. Richard Dawkins, *River Out of Eden* (London: Orion, 1996).
2. Franklin Graham (Ed.), *Billy Graham in Quotes,* (Nashville: Thomas Nelson, 2011).
3. Paul David Tripp, *Instruments in the Redeemer's Hands,* (Phillipsburg, NJ: P&R Publishing, 2002), 143.
4. U.S. Census Bureau, *Disability*, www.census.gov/people/disabiliy/ (March, 2017).
5. World Health Organization, *Disabilities*, www.who.int/topics/disabilities/en/ (November, 2017).
6. Michael R. Emlet, *Descriptions and Prescriptions,* (Greensboro, NC: New Growth Press, 2017), 11.
7. Robin S. Rosenberg, *Abnormal is the New Normal,* www.slate.com/articles/ (April 12, 2013).
8. Emlet, *Descriptions and Prescriptions*, 46.
9. Craig Ferguson, *American on Purpose,* (New York City: Harper Perennial, 2010).
10. ADHD World Federation, *A Short History of ADHD,* www.adhd-federation.org/adhd-world-federation/short-history-on-adhd/ (November, 2017).
11. The Ehlers-Danlos Society, *What are the Ehlers-Danlos Syndromes?* www.ehlers-danlos.com/what-is-eds/ (November, 2017).
12. Tara Haelle, *Many Young Adults With Autism Also Have Mental Health Issues*, www.npr.org/sections/health-shots/2017/10/01/55461501/many-young-adults-with-autism-also-have-mental-health-issues (October 1, 2017).
13. Haelle, *Many Young Adults.*
14. Amanda MacMillan, *Why Mental Illness Can Fuel Physical Disease*, www.time.com/4679492/depression-anxiety-chronic-disease/ , (February 23, 2017).
15. Edward T Welch, Blame it on the Brain, (Phillipsburg, NJ: P&R Publishing, 1998), 106.
16. Elyse Fitzpatrick and Laura Hendrickson, *Will Medicine Stop the Pain?* (Chicago: Moody Publishers, 2006). 85.
17. Joni Eareckson Tada, *A Place of Healing,* (Colorado Springs, CO: David C. Cook, 2010), 101.

18. Michael S. Beates, *Disability and the Gospel,* (Wheaton, IL: Crossway, 2012), 140.
19. Bob Smietana, *Mental Illness Remains Taboo Topic for Many Pastors,* www.lifewayresearch.com/2014/09/22/mental-illness-remains-taboo-topic-for-many-pastors/ (September 22, 2014).
20. Timothy Keller, *The Gospel in Life: Grace Changes Everything, Study Guide,* (Grand Rapids, MI: Zondervan, 2010).
21. Jeff McNair, *The weblog disabled Christianity: The Church and Disability,* (CreateSpace, 2010), 31.
22. Timothy Keller, *Counterfeit Gods,* (Westminster, UK: Penguin Books, 2011), 172.
23. John Dos Passos, *The Prospect Before Us,* (Boston, MA: Houghton Mifflin, 1950).
24. Brad Hambrick, *Five Ways the Church Can Help Someone Facing Mental Illness,* www.elrc.com/resource-library/articles/5-ways-the-church-can-help-someone-facing-mental-illness, (June 8, 2015).
25. Edward T. Welch, *Side by Side,* (Wheaton, IL: Crossway, 2015), 15.
26. Tripp, *Instruments,* 145.
27. Joni Eareckson Tada, Interview.
28. Amos Yong, *The Bible, Disability, and the Church,* (Grand Rapids, MI: Eerdmans, 2011), 95.
29. Tripp, *Instruments,* 145.
30. Beates, *Disability and the Gospel,* 79.
31. Rob Moss, *Why we will no longer be a Welcoming Church,* www.livinglutheran.org/2016/06/will-no-longer-welcoming-church/ (June 22, 2016).
32. Yong, *The Bible, Disability, and the Church,* 108.
33. Tripp, *Instruments,* 153.
34. (Acronym for Mobile Army Surgical Hospital—an American war comedy-drama television series that aired on CBS from 1972 to 1983)
35. www.etymonline.com/index.php?term=hospital.
36. Christine D. Pohl, *Living into Community,* (Grand Rapids, MI: Eerdmans, 2011), 159.
37. Pohl, *Living into Community,* 165.
38. Tim Chester and Steve Timmis, *Total Church,* (Wheaton, IL: Crossway, 2008), 41.
39. Yong, *The Bible, Disability, and the Church,* 115.
40. www.etymonline.com/word/familiar.
41. Julianne Holt-Lunstad, *So Lonely I Could Die,* www.apa.org/news/press/releases/2017/08/lonely-die.aspx, (August 5, 2017).
42. www.stlyrics.com/lyrics/televisiontvthemelyrics-80s90s/cheers.htm.
43. Shoba Sreenivasan and Linda E. Weinberger, *Why We Need Each Other,* www.psychology.com/blog/emotional-nourishment/201612/why-we-need-each-other, (December 14, 2016).

44. Timothy S. Lane and Paul David Tripp, *How People Change*, (Greensboro, NC: New Growth Press, 2008), 74.
45. Bob Smietana, *Mental Illness Remains Taboo Topic for Many Pastors*, www.lifewayresearch.com/2014/09/22/mental-illness-remains-taboo-topic-for-many-pastors/ (September 22, 2014).
46. Robyn Henderson-Espinoza, *The Silent Stigma of Mental Illness in the Church*, www.sojo.net/articles/silent-stigma-mental-illness-church, (May 10, 2017).
47. Debra Kirouac, *Alone in the Crowd: The Pain of Social Exclusion*, www.news.bridgeport.edu/breakthroughs/alone-in-the-crowd-the-pain-of-social-exclusion (August 15, 2016).
48. McNair, *The Church and Disability*, 200.
49. McNair, *The Church and Disability*, 200.
50. www.en.oxforddictionaries.com/definition/respite.
51. Stephanie O. Hubach, *Same Lake, Different Boat: Coming Alongside People Touched by Disability*, (Phillipsburg, NJ:P&R Publishing, 2006), 182.
52. Chester and Timmis, *Total Church*.
53. Timothy Keller, *Walking with God Through Pain and Suffering*, (Westminster, UK: Penguin Books, 2011), 308.
54. Mark Dever, *What is a Healthy Church?* (Wheaton, IL: Crossway, 2007), 111.
55. Mark Dever and Paul Alexander, *The Deliberate Church*, (Wheaton, IL: Crossway, 2005), 38.
56. Garrett Higbee, "Biblical Counseling and Soul Care in the Church," in *Biblical Counseling and the Church*, (Grand Rapids, MI: Zondervan, 2015), 65.
57. Jeremy Pierre and Deepak Reju, *The Pastor and Counseling*, (Wheaton, IL: Crossway, 2005), 114-115.
58. www.etymonline.com/index.php?term=educate.
59. Pierre and Reju, *The Pastor and Counseling*, 107.
60. Pierre and Reju, *The Pastor and Counseling*, 106.
61. Robert W. Kellemen, *Equipping Counselors for your Church*, (Phillipsburg, NJ: P&R Publishing, 2011), 35.
62. William W. Goode, "Biblical Counseling in the Local Church," in *Counseling: How to Counsel Biblically,"* (Nashville, TN: Thomas Nelson, 2005), 226.
63. Smietana, *Mental Illness Remains Taboo Topic for Many Pastors*.
64. Higbee, "Biblical Counseling and Soul Care in the Church," 58.
65. Kellemen, *Equipping Counselors*, 36.
66. John Piper, *"Don't Waste Your Cancer,"* www.desiringgod.org/articles/dont-waste-your-cancer, February 15, 2006.

OTHER BOOKS BY SHEPHERD PRESS

(See the following pages.)

Treasure in the Ashes:
Our Journey Home from the Ruins of Sexual Abuse

Sue Nicewander and Maria Brookins
Trade Paperback, 368pp
ISBN: 978-1-63342-139-4

Treasure in the Ashes is an interactive book that gently leads readers on a biblical journey through the grueling questions and doubt, emotional turmoil, and relational fallout that follows sexual abuse.

Sue Nicewander, MABC, ACBC, BCC, has been counseling since 1994. She is founder and training coordinator of Biblical Counseling Ministries, Wisconsin Rapids, Wisconsin, and serves on the Council Board of the Biblical Counseling Coalition. Sue has her MA in biblical counseling from Central Baptist Theological Seminary. Sue and her late husband Jim were married for 43 years. The Nicewander family includes two beautiful married daughters and six delightful grandchildren.

Maria Brookins has a BS in Biblical Studies/Counseling from Faith Baptist Bible College in Ankeny, Iowa. She and her husband, Corey, have been serving together in ministry since 2004. They enjoy God's gift of a full and vibrant life with four fabulous boys and two crazy dogs.

"I'm thankful for this resource. I'm sure you will be, too."
—*Elyse M. Fitzpatrick*

"I pray this book finds its way into the hands of everyone who has undergone the wretched experience of sexual abuse."
—*Curtis W. Solomon*

DISCIPLING THE FLOCK: A CALL TO FAITHFUL SHEPHERDING

Paul Tautges
Trade Paperback, 96pp
ISBN: 978-1-63342-142-4

Here is an urgent appeal to return to authentic discipleship; here is a call to shepherds to be tenacious in their preaching of the whole counsel of God, and tender in their application of its truth to the lives of God's sheep through personal ministry.

Author Paul Tautges has been in gospel ministry since 1992 and currently serves as senior pastor of Cornerstone Community Church (EFCA) in Cleveland, Ohio. Paul is the author of many books including *Comfort the Grieving*, *Counseling One Another*, and *Pray about Everything*, and serves as the series editor for the LifeLine mini-books. He is also an adjunct professor and blogs at CounselingOneAnother.com.

"Here is an anchor for authentic ministry that will stimulate real spiritual growth in God's people." —Dr. Steven J. Lawson

"... this book gets it right." —John MacArthur

"...a biblically faithful, practically helpful guide to find the important balance between the public and private ministry of the Word of God..."

—Brian Croft, Senior Pastor,
Auburndale Baptist Church, Louisville, Kentucky

COUNSEL WITH CONFIDENCE:
A QUICK REFERENCE GUIDE
FOR BIBLICAL COUNSELORS AND DISCIPLERS

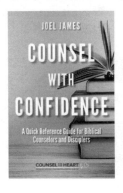

Joel James
Trade paperback, 224pp
ISBN: 978-1-63342-148-6

When you were learning to ride a bicycle, the hardest part was the first few pedal strokes—those wobbly seconds before you built up enough momentum to maintain your balance. A generous push from your dad was just what you needed to avoid ending up in a heap of elbows, knees, handlebars, and spokes. Counseling is similar. Sometimes you need something to give you some momentum, something to give you the confidence that you're on the right track. If you've ever felt like that, this book is for you.

Author Joel James has an M.Div. and a D.Min. from The Master's Seminary and is the pastor-teacher of Grace Fellowship in Pretoria, South Africa. He and his wife, Ruth, have been married since 1993 and have two children.

COUNSELING ONE ANOTHER:
A THEOLOGY OF INTERPERSONAL DISCIPLESHIP

Paul Tautges
Trade paperback, 192pp
ISBN: 978-1-63342-094-6

A book to help believers understand the process of being transformed by God's grace and truth

"This book gets it right! Comprehensive and convincing, Counseling One Another *shows how true biblical counseling and preaching fit hand-in-glove. Those who preach, teach or counsel regularly are sure to benefit greatly from this helpful resource."*

—Dr. John MacArthur, Pastor-Teacher,
Grace Community Church,
President, The Master's University and Seminary

"Paul Tautges lays the theological foundation for biblical counseling— in a way that is both comprehensive and compassionate. This book demonstrates a staunch commitment to an expository, exegetical examination of counseling as presented in God's Word. Any pastor or lay person wanting a foundational starting point for understanding Christ-centered, comprehensive, and compassionate biblical counseling in the local church would be wise to read and reread Counseling One Another.*"*

—Bob Kellemen,
Executive Director of The Biblical Counseling Coalition

LIFELINE MINI-BOOKS

(See the following pages.)

The LifeLine mini-books address day-to-day issues from a Bible-centered perspective, with an emphasis on bringing help and guidance to people who are struggling or suffering, as well as to those who minister to them. Produced under the editorial direction of Dr. Paul Tautges, these resources include a clear gospel presentation, personal application projects, and a list of further resources. Each mini-book is pocket sized (6 x 4 inches) and 64 pages in extent. Quantity discounts available. More info at: www.lifelineminibooks.com.

> "These little books are directly targeted to the issues that we all face and they hit the bulls-eye. They are faithful to Scripture and demonstrate insight into its application. Churches need to make these available for their congregations."
>
> —John MacArthur,
> Pastor-Teacher, Grace Community Church;
> President, The Master's University and Seminary

> "Many Christian counselors are seeking helpful material that is faithful to the Scriptures. The LifeLine mini-book series is an invaluable tool in their counseling tool kit because it will genuinely help struggling Christians with practical answers that are true to the sufficient Word of God."
>
> —Dr. John Street,
> Chair of MABC program,
> The Master's University, Santa Clarita, CA

> "These books demonstrate that biblical counsel can be made simple without becoming shallow. There is real meat here: robust analysis, honest assessment, rich gospel application and practical steps, all delivered in tidy mini-books that will not be overwhelming to God's people."
>
> —Tedd Tripp, Author, Speaker
> Director of Shepherd Press

(List of Lifeline mini-books overleaf.)

LifeLine mini-books

Many more LifeLine mini-books are in preparation!

About Shepherd Press Publications

- They are gospel driven.
- They are heart focused.
- They are life changing.

Our Invitation to You

We passionately believe that what we are publishing can be of benefit to you, your family, your friends, and your work colleagues. So we are inviting you to join our online mailing list so that we may reach out to you with news about our latest and forthcoming publications, and with special offers.

Visit:

www.shepherdpress.com/newsletter

and provide your name and email address.